T5-ASM-869

THE SPHINX AWAKES

THE SPHINX AWAKES

by

GERALD SPARROW

Author of "Land of the Moonflower"

ILLUSTRATED

ROBERT HALE LIMITED

63 Old Brompton Road London S.W.7

First published 1956

PRINTED IN GREAT BRITAIN BY
NORTHUMBERLAND PRESS LIMITED
GATESHEAD ON TYNE

CONTENTS

APPENDICES

To

CAMBRIDGE

WHERE I FIRST LEARNT THESE THINGS

ILLUSTRATIONS

FOREWORD

As I write this Britain and Egypt are passing through a crisis as strange and difficult as any in their tortuous history.

Intensely proud as I am of Britain and of the Commonwealth countries, I still am perturbed by the amount of distortion and prejudice that, with some notable exceptions, has crept into newspapers both in London and in Cairo.

Middle-aged men and women of my generation are now being accused by young men and women between the ages of seventeen and twenty-five of mismanaging international affairs to an intolerable extent during the last four decades. I feel that charge justified. Nor do I think we can answer it adequately by pointing out that, fifteen years ago, when we ourselves were younger, we helped to save the world from the hideous fate of German and Japanese domination.

One of the things we could do to improve our record would be fully to understand the resurgent movement of the Arab States, linked as they are by ties of faith, language and self-interest.

If we are able to go further and, by our fairness, firmness and friendship, guide this dynamic movement into profitable and peaceful paths we shall have done something to rebutt the verdict of our sons and daughters which seems to be that we have the stench of death about us and are for ever whining about Hitler.

The Arab and Islamic Revolution, on an international scale, is going to effect our lives for many years to come. I hope that this book, by catching and holding the reader's interest, may play its modest, but useful, part in helping both generations to understand this new and exciting development.

GERALD SPARROW.

Blackheath.

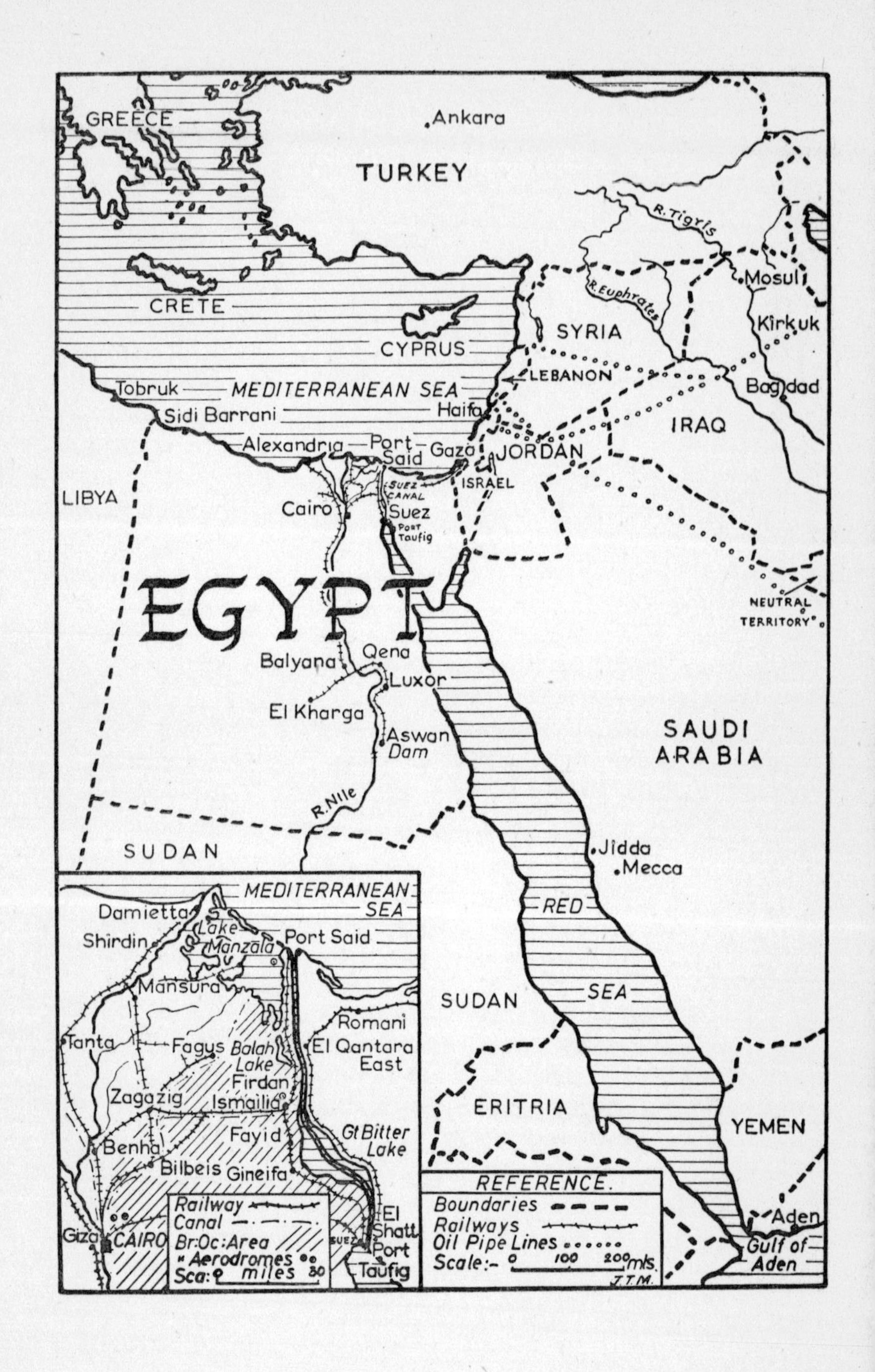

GREECE
Ankara
TURKEY
R. Tigris
R. Euphrates
Mosul
Kirkuk
CRETE
CYPRUS
SYRIA
LEBANON
Bagdad
Tobruk
MEDITERRANEAN SEA
Sidi Barrani
Haifa
IRAQ
Alexandria
Port Said
Gaza
JORDAN
ISRAEL
LIBYA
SUEZ CANAL
Cairo
Suez
Port Taufig
NEUTRAL TERRITORY
EGYPT
Balyana
Qena
Luxor
El Kharga
Aswan Dam
SAUDI ARABIA
R. Nile
SUDAN
Jidda
Mecca
RED
SEA
SUDAN
ERITRIA
YEMEN
Aden
Gulf of Aden
MEDITERRANEAN SEA
Damietta
Shirdin
Lake Manzala
Port Said
Mansura
Romani
Tanta
Fagus
Balah Lake
El Qantara East
Firdan
Zagazig
Ismailia
Fayid
Gt Bitter Lake
Benha
Bilbeis
Gineifa
El Shatt
Giza
CAIRO
SUEZ
Port Taufig
Railway
Canal
Br:Oc:Area
Aerodromes
Sca: 0 miles 30
REFERENCE.
Boundaries
Railways
Oil Pipe Lines
Scale:- 0 100 200 mls.
J.T.M.

CHAPTER ONE

CURTAIN RAISER

IT was April in London, but it was still cold, changeable, the sky smiling and frowning like a spoilt débutante. I had three calls to make: the first at 75 South Audley Street, the Egyptian Embassy, the second at the Foreign Office in Downing Street, and the third at the Egyptian State Tourist Office in Piccadilly. For to-morrow I should be off. My spirits rose at the thought.

I have always loved travel for its own sake, air travel in particular. Business and pleasure have taken me a hundred thousand miles by air in the eleven years since I released myself from a Japanese prison camp, years in which fortune had smiled on me as a lawyer, so that now I am able to retire and devote my time to writing. I am still exhilarated by the change. For ten years I had shuffled papers, argued on documents, negotiated and pleaded in my international practice, shuttling between the Far East, London and New York. Now all that is over. I am free to put life on paper—if I can.

Nearly every journey I make seems to take me through Cairo, and always, if I can, I linger, fascinated by the people, by their fantastically preserved history, their unique situation and their problems.

The personality of King Farouk itself was a challenge. He slept for very short periods, being one of the most restless of men, constantly on the move. After his fall we knew that his palace contained vast collections in exquisite taste, but the taste was that of a small coterie of the King's staff, who grew rich through his purchases. The King, himself, in his private apartments at the Kubbeh Gardens Palace, mixed vulgar modern designs with fine furniture and ceramics quite happily. His wealth was fabulous, but he was careful even with his relatives and friends. When he married Queen Narriman he insisted on all the official wedding presents being made of gold. On the 26th of July, 1952, at the Ras El-Tin

Palace, he wrote in his own hand the short abdication rescript beginning: "Whereas we always seek the welfare of our people and cherish their happiness and prosperity. . . ." He started his reign most auspiciously, young and loved. He ended it in failure.

Then, out of the blue, suddenly, the Army revolt broke. After General Neguib's short interlude, Gamal Abdel Nasser became supreme commander of all Egypt. Egypt, according to Mr. Gunther, was "laid open like a rotten melon". I find the trend of the foreign comment on the new Egypt too slick, too anxious to be in the swim. Gunther, one of the best of the commentators, puts it like this: "It would be a tragic day for Egypt and the world if this Revolution was to be overturned and the country should succumb to forces more revolutionary (Communism?) or, worse, be sucked back into the sloth, greed and infamy of the old régime." I feel that this is too easy, unworthy of the real issues at stake.

Before I wrote a word on Egypt I was determined to enlist the aid of those Egyptians who, by training, experience and inclination, would be able to tell me what I still did not know about their country. I have studied Egypt since I was a youth, but there were many aspects of the 1952 Revolution that puzzled me. Was this merely an Army revolt against the Crown, or was it a true political, economic and social revolution? I meant to find out. Hence my visits to the Embassy, and the Foreign Office.

In South Audley Street a butler who resembled my idea of a Roman Senator—he had, I think what the Romans called "gravitas" —received me, and showed me into a reception-room of Homeric proportions, furnished entirely in red and gold. The carpet, which ran the whole length of the room, was a thing of real beauty and magnificence. The one painting on the wall, a Cairo market scene, was colourful, but had little sense of perspective or composition. Two young Egyptians were drinking coffee and going through a pile of correspondence at the far end of the room. They spoke in undertones and not a word of their conversation reached me. The doors opened and the First Secretary came in. Moustafa El-Dib Benshi is a man in the late thirties. He looks not unlike the press photographs of Prince Ranier of Monaco, and is equally cosmopolitan. He speaks excellent English. Talking to him it occurred to me that he had the heart of an Egyptian but the mind of a Frenchman. He was polished, polite, helpful, encouraging.

He wrote out for me, on handsome Egyptian Embassy stationery, three private letters of introduction. They were most generously worded. I glanced at the name on the envelope—His Excellency the Under-Secretary, Ministry of National Guidance, Cairo; the Director-General of the Publicity Bureau; the third was a personal friend of Mr. Benshi's.

"These people can arrange everything for you, yes, even meetings with the Premier, who is very busy just now. We have nothing to hide." Mr. Benshi looked out of the window at the cold, blustering weather and added with a smile: "How I wish I were coming with you—into the sun again."

I thanked him sincerely. The Embassy could not have been more helpful. There was no suspicion, no distrust, they had only shown a genuine desire to help so that I really could become informed of the inside story of the Revolution and be able to tell that story well.

I motored back past the Palace. The daffodils were out defying the elements, making a brave yellow splash in Pall Mall. I turned right past the Horse Guards Parade into Whitehall and Downing Street. A small crowd had gathered opposite Number Ten waiting, I think, for Sir Anthony Eden to receive some visitors. They parted to let me turn in under the arches to the Foreign Office Courtyard. In the reception office one of the three ladies who work there rang the Egyptian Department. "Judge Sparrow is here, and would like to come up." Apparently the answer was favourable for the young woman said: "Will you sit down a moment? I'll send for a messenger to conduct you."

I sat waiting, studying the fine portrait of Lord Salisbury on the wall to the right and the magnificent Chinese screen, the gift, in 1896, of Li Hung Chang, the last great Foreign Minister of Imperial China. History has accumulated here, and left behind a golden dust of knowledge and decorum.

In less than two minutes the blue-liveried porter appeared. He glanced at a piece of green paper the receptionist had handed him. "To see Mr. Hardwick, sir, yes. Please come with me."

He knocked at a room far down one of the dark stone corridors. Several men were working in the room, most of them seemed quite young. As I turned into the room I passed a desk labelled "High Dam". I was in the midst of official British contacts with the new Egypt. There was very little conversation in the room, but occasionally one of the young men would toss a paper, with a smile, to another. I had the feeling they all knew each other, and were a fraternity.

Mr. Hardwick was as frank and helpful as the Egyptians had been. He handed over a large amount of material on aspects of the new Egypt he thought might interest British and American readers. He was a tall, dark, young man with a very high, protruding forehead. I asked him about Colonel Nasser.

"Well, you know, we are having second thoughts about him. If we can get a common Russian-British-American agreement to prevent the outbreak of a war between Egypt and Israel, then we may be able to win Nasser as a friend, and persuade him to stop his plotting which is causing us so much damage—but at present we go ahead and strengthen our Baghdad Pact."

"What do the British statesmen think of Colonel Nasser?"

"As far as I know all our Ministers, except one, have been impressed by his sincerity, energy and charm." He paused; I had the impression he was going to tell me who the one important exception was, but his training was too strong. He smiled, but said no more.

I gathered the papers he had prepared for me, thanked him, and was leaving as he said: "We shall be interested to hear your impressions when you return."

I said I should certainly like another talk with him then. I passed through the line of desks and had the distinct impression that one of the young gentlemen had made a note of my name and personal appearance. I wondered what he had noted. "Gerald Sparrow, retired Judge from Bangkok, International lawyer. Late forties, red hair, blue eyes, over six foot tall, with a dominant, hooked nose. Fairly U." Something like that had, I think, been scribbled on a memorandum.

My last port of call was the Egyptian State Tourist Office in Piccadilly. This was a change after the Georgian and Victorian dimness of the Foreign Office. The Tourist Office was modern, almost futuristic in its architecture, design and furnishing. I sat on a steel-and-glass chair chatting to Mr. Khalid Azmy, who was described politely on his card as Tourist Attaché. With us was Mr. M. K. Handy, whom Mr. Azmy described as "my assistant Director".

They were both neat, dapper little men and spoke tolerable English.

"Yes, the Ministry of National Guidance will, of course, give you all the information you require. We can help with photographs for your book." Mr. Azmy beckoned to his colleague, who went to a bureau and produced some fine photographs of the Egyptian scene. To sustain the conversation I said how pathetically little most of us knew of the people of other countries, even of countries like Egypt, only ten hours distant by air.

Mr. Azmy agreed enthusiastically. "I go," he said, "to cocktail parties and the ladies come up to me and say: tell me, please, how you train your crocodiles on the Nile. Don't you find the camels very difficult in the Cairo traffic?" Mr. Azmy smiled a little forlornly. "I tell them that—especially since the Revolution—we are a modern, progressive people with 5,000 years of intense civilization. It makes no difference. It's always the same, camels and crocodiles."

For a moment I had the fleeting, irreverent impression that Mr. Azmy and Mr. Handy were a pair of charming, diplomatic comedians, with the sad smiles of perpetual disillusion that all true comedians have.

"Anything we can do to help. We shall be delighted. Please remember this office. Have you our names spelt correctly? Yes? Good-bye. Enjoy yourself in Cairo."

Out in the traffic-laden street I realized that the Egyptian State Tourist Office had a flavour and charm of its own.

I picked up my Austin, which I had parked in Air Street (there is usually three vacant yards opposite the theatre agency) and collected my air ticket in Jermyn Street. Next morning I was at London Airport long before it was necessary to catch the Air France plane. I have always envied, but never been able to emulate, the split-second plane-catchers. I decided to break the journey and stay overnight in Paris at the little hotel in the Rue Fontaine. Before the British had ruled in Egypt Napoleon Bonaparte had gone there and conquered. At least some recent Egyptian roots were in Paris. I thought it would do no harm if I tasted, once again, the tang of the Paris streets—and some exquisite cooking—before I moved on next morning, still by Air France, to Cairo.

That evening I revived my memories of Paris, ending in Montmartre with friends in the early morning. In Paris there is a conspiracy to entertain you at all hours, just as in London there is a conspiracy to get you home by midnight. I contrived to get five hours sleep and again reached the airport much too early.

It was an uneventful flight. Air France gave us aperitifs, champagne, and liqueurs at frequent intervals so that the passengers were soon in a happy, carefree, lethargic state. They were nearly all French. There was one Englishwoman, about my own age. She looked as if she was about to step on to the first tee at Sunningdale.

It was not until the evening that we started to lose height; descending to two thousand feet as we passed over the Egyptian coastline that shimmered, golden and iridescent, in the evening sun. On we went towards Cairo and I saw again the man-made mountain tombs, the eternal wonder of the Pyramids.

We landed gracefully, skilfully. This was the airport I remembered as Farouk Airport. It was "Cairo Airport" now. I said good-bye to the hostess who spoke English with that delightful hesitancy that adds charm to the most mundane conversation of French women. I thanked the Captain for so smooth and happy a voyage. Then I took a taxi to my hotel, the Metropolitan, recommended me by my Egyptian friends.

That night, dining alone, I looked through my stack of introductory letters that included some distinguished foreign correspondents, and some of our resident diplomats. I decided then and there to base my book, in so far as I could, on Egyptian information and contacts, only bringing in outside criticism if experience and knowledge told me that the Egyptian story was misleading on account of partiality and prejudice.

I listened to the conversation around me. Three languages, Arabic, French, and English were competing to dominate the conversational scene. Occasionally French or English seemed to assert itself, but on the whole the chant and hiss of Arabic drowned the foreign invaders.

I retired early to my bedroom, a neat, air-conditioned room, one of two hundred similar chambers. Over the wash-stand basin hung a photograph of the new leader. Underneath was written in English and Arabic "His Excellency Colonel Gamal Abdel Nasser, Leader of Egypt". I looked at the long, dark face, aggressive, lively, handsome, and wondered what sort of a man this really was. And,

The imposing new Shepheards Hotel

The new Ottoman Bank building in Cairo

Kasr El Nil Street—Mostafu Kamel Square

as I threw off my clothes, I prayed that I might have the gift to paint a true, understanding account of these people as they really were, not as foreigners see them, but as Allah made them.

NOTE. Readers who are allergic to history, in any form, may omit chapter two. On the other hand the golden glories and black troughs of Egyptian history have a curiously intimate connection with what is now happening in Arab countries. Colonel Nasser's mentality, the attitude of all Egyptians, and the bold dream of a great New Arab Union, all have their roots in what has gone before. Chapter two is an attempt to turn the pages of the past as painlessly as possible.

CHAPTER TWO

WHAT WENT BEFORE

As soon as I started an intensive study of the Egyptian scene in Cairo, I knew that the Revolution of July 23rd had been a deeper, more radical business than I had realized.

Not only was the Mahomet Aly Dynasty ended, but the whole tenor and pattern of life in Egypt was altered, or subject to new pressures. The heroes of yesterday were the villains of to-day.

The Egyptian Press, with remarkable agility, dropped their Royalist cloak and came out in favour of the Revolution.

The proposed land reforms promised to change the economic life of the people, bringing the fellaheen from feudalism to modernity, while a two-chambered parliament and new constitution, if it became fully operative, would profoundly affect the political rights and liberties of Egyptians as a whole.

So, at first, it seemed that I might conveniently start this account during the early night hours of July 23rd, 1952, when the weeks of plotting ended in the Army taking over. But, on reflection, this was not feasible. However much the political leaders may wish to alter the society they control, the people have roots in the past that even they cannot sever. A nation has grown up through the centuries, a a national character has been been formed, a tradition and pattern of life created. I must, therefore, very briefly, tell the Egyptian story from the start. Then the reason for the Revolution, and its soaring ambitions at home and abroad, will be seen in truer perspective.

Recent excavations in Egypt, delving deep into her ancient history, are again capturing world imagination, as similar works did when the fantastic tomb of Tutankamen was uncovered in 1922.

The Pyramids and the Sphinx are known throughout the world but, long before these vast monuments were built, Egypt was already an organized state with a complex civilization, a major factor in the progress of humanity, in learning, and a great influence—even at that time, in the ancient East.

Without going back to pre-historic or pre-dynastic times, the Egypt of about 3,000 B.C. is a fascinating picture. The land, then, from the Mediterranean to the far South was united under one ruler. He was known at the King of Upper and Lower Egypt; his crown bore the symbol of "The Two Lands". Mena, the founder of the First Dynasty, chose the site for Egypt's capital at the apex of the Nile Delta. To create his new city, Memphis, he diverted the river and reclaimed the marshlands.

Through these years great strides were made in the development of writing, the principles of which were already known at the beginning of the period. The development of early Egyptian art can be traced through archaeological material brought to light, and in this First Dynasty it had been mastered and the wonderful edifices were erected that have since excited and awed the world.

The Third Dynasty began about the year 2,700 B.C. and with the capital now firmly established in the North. King Zoser built the famous Step Pyramid at Sakkara—the earliest large stone building in the world, which is surrounded by remains of many stone structures of smaller size of the same period.[1]

Egypt produced a man of genius very early in its known history, a man of humble family possessing great talents and energy that moved him to the forefront of affairs and soon placed him second only to the King. This was the mighty Imhotep[2], the minor official who startled Egypt and whose memory has been preserved in Egyptian history until modern times. 2,500 years after his death, he was still worshipped as a God in Egypt. Temples were erected to do him honour as the God of Medicine and the God who knew all the secrets of all Gods.

Before the coming of Imhotep, kings were buried in large rectangular buildings known now as mastabas. Imhotep did not think this fitting for kingly honour and his idea was the construction of mastabas each on top of another, decreasing in size as they ascended, until the final structure resulted in pyramid form. Without doubt, Imhotep was one of the greatest builders of ancient Egypt and was directly responsible for the astonishing development of Egyptian architecture which followed the building of the Step Pyramid. King Snefru carried the advance further.

In the Fourth Dynasty, Snefru had several pyramids erected,

[1] These are now in the Cairo Museum.

[2] Colonel Nasser is a great admirer of Imhotep.

including the Southern Pyramid at Dahshsur, which was the first attempt at attaining the true pyramidal form on a square base. Reliefs and statues from the Valley Temple of the period show to-day the excellence of the art of the period with a style and technique hardly surpassed by any other period in Egyptian history.

Snefru was a benevolent king, a patron of the arts, a wise administrator. It was he who sent a fleet to Lebanon for cedar wood beams, some of which have since been found intact inside an excavated pyramid[1]. Monuments to Snefru and his Queen have survived 4,500 years after his death.

The school of builders which Snefru founded was responsible for the Great Pyramid—one of the Seven Wonders of the World in olden times and one of the great masterpieces of human engineering skill to-day.

The Sphinx no longer has her secret. Excavations and research have shown that the Sphinx was cut from solid stone in the time of King Khafra and was considered to be his own statue: the human head and lion's body being the combination of human wisdom and physical strength. It was only in the Eighteenth Dynasty—that is, the fifteenth century B.C.—that the ancient Egyptians regarded the Sphinx as the symbol of the God Horemakhet, the rising sun.

The Fifth Dynasty saw the erection of the Temple of the Sun God, a huge obelisk rising to the sky. From this dynasty we can catch a further glimpse of ancient civilization, for stone pictures have been discovered showing the rich man listening to music, welcoming guests, inspecting estates, and hunting. There are representations of the ancient market place, the shoppers, the merchants at work, the bakers and the goldsmiths.[2]

Later Egypt's influence, especially upon culture, spread across all Syria and Palestine and into Crete and Cyprus,[3] but after this glorious period, there ensued another collapse. The tide of greatness ebbed and, for two centuries, Egypt was a land of chaos and fell victim to foreign invasion by a race whom the ancient Egyptian had

[1] Sir Winston Churchill makes this lively comparison between ancient Britain and Egypt in his *History of the English-speaking Peoples*.

"Britain was still little more than a promontory of Europe, or divided from it by a narrow tide race which has gradually enlarged into the Straits of Dover, when the Pyramids were a-building, and when learned Egyptians were laboriously exploring the ancient ruins of Sakkara."

[2] The Fifth Dynasty seems to have been as "civilized" as eighteenth century England.

[3] Colonel Nasser keeps a watch on Cyprus, following events there, day by day.

styled the Hyksos. They occupied the Nile Delta for over a hundred years, forcing the rulers of Upper Egypt to pay them tribute. The national spirit of Egypt was not, however, killed. The humiliation of foreign rule bred patriotism.

The Theban Princes rose against the Hyksos in a war of independence and the invaders were thrown out of Egypt. The foreign army installed itself, after flight, in Palestine; but a three year siege caused the collapse of this garrison. Egypt was again restored as a great imperial power.

The ruling house of the Eighteenth Dynasty held sway between 1,570 and 1,320 B.C., during which time this family of warriors steadily expanded the Egyptian empire to embrace all the then known East. One of the kings of this period, Thotmose III, was a master strategist. His genius has been a model for many more modern military strategists. The famous campaign to Megiddo of Thotmose III was copied by General Allenby in the First World War. This King undertook sixteen campaigns and introduced into Egypt many hitherto unknown plants and animals, including the domestic chicken and the pomegranate from Syria.

Thebes became the capital of this ancient world, the meeting place of envoys from all over the East bringing gifts to Egypt as tribute. Thotmose III was succeeded by a warrior son—Amenhotep II—who excelled in physical strength and sports.

The luxury and love of building great monuments probably reached its zenith during the reign of another Amenhotep—the Third. He left fabulous monuments and had a great son—Akhenaton—who was one of the outstanding men of the ancient world. Akhenaton addressed hymns to one God of all the universe and fought against the theory of numerous deities. His life was directed towards freedom, urging his people to free themselves from the bonds and fetters of tradition whenever and wherever they found them. His beautiful queen was Nefertiti, but he left no male heir and his kingdom was in the throes of trouble. His two daughters wed two young princes, one of them the Tutankamen whose tomb as late as 1922 was found containing the magnificent treasures and artistic wealth which are now the glory of the Cairo Museum.

This Eighteenth Dynasty, which lasted for a period of 250 years, started in glory and ended in glory with an interim period of revolt and trouble.

The Nineteenth Dynasty started with the firm rule of a general, one chosen by the people themselves—Rameses. He founded a new royal house and embellished the old city in the Delta. His son, Sety, matched his father's greatness, proving a worthy successor to the great Thotmose III. Sety made the kingdom rich and prosperous, started the exploitation of mines in the desert, built temples of unsurpassed beauty, including the gem at Abydos.

Rameses II followed him and earned the reputation as the most popular of Egyptian Kings.

Rameses reigned for sixty-seven years and there are few ancient places in Egypt which do not bear his name on some of their monuments—the temples of Karnak and Luxor and the great rock cut temples of Abu Simbel in Nubia are among the most famous which survive to-day and thrill visitors with their grandeur.

An ancient granite statue of Rameses II weighing more than seventy tons, which for years has been resting in a horizontal position at Badreshein, is now being moved into Cairo. It will be re-erected in one of the capital's principal squares, near the main station, as a symbol of Egypt's proud past.

Under Rameses II, Egypt repelled invasion, especially from the sea. This was about 1,200 B.C. and a period in which the wars of Troy were raging and when the first battles between Egypt and the peoples of Europe were recorded. These records were discovered in the Temple of Medinet Habu. The dynasty saw the struggle of the priesthood to seize power. The priests had, through the years, become immensely wealthy. Priests of Amon owned one-tenth of all cultivated land, huge herds of cattle, gold mines and whole towns at home and abroad. Weak kings gave the priests their opportunity and finally the Priest of Amon was able to declare himself Pharaoh. A period of decline then set in as the priest kings held sway and attempted revivals of the old spirit failed to achieve permanence.

When the rule of the priests ended in the Twenty-first Dynasty, another royal house arose which forced the priests southwards. They set up a rule in the Sudan, claimed the kingdom of Kush and proclaimed themselves as legal heirs to the throne of Thebes and all Egypt. But Pinakhi put an end to the dynasts and forced the country to accept him as king. His line flourished through the years and his son was Taharka, who is a figure in the Book of Kings in the Old Testament.

Assyria in this period was bent upon expansion and military collisions occurred between her and the forces of Egypt and Syria. In these troubled days one of the great houses in the western Delta decided to try to unite the country. They realized their goal. Greece was playing her part in world history during this epoch and the Kings of the Twenty-sixth Dynasty employed Greek mercenaries in their armies and encouraged Greek merchants and scholars to stay in Egypt. A real renaissance was under way and the period restored the former glories of the land. Greek philosophers came to Egypt and gained entry into the temples and began their learning from these temples, which they afterwards acknowledged in their many writings.[1]

Trading expanded as Egypt improved her position at the centre of the known world and as the meeting point between Europe, Asia and Africa. Herodotus, the Greek historian, recorded how one of the kings of this period—Nekaw—sent a naval expedition to explore the coast of all Africa. They went sailing down the Red Sea and after a three year voyage returned to Egypt again at the Mediterranean coast. Nekaw also attempted to connect the Mediterranean with the Red Sea by a canal. It was not a new idea. Such a canal had once been built and used, in the Eighteenth Dynasty, but had subsequently become silted up. Nekaw set out upon his project but when it was about half completed, an oracle from the Temple of Bute ordered work to cease. The oracle had declared the scheme harmful to the national interests and said only Egypt's enemies, the barbarians, would profit from it. In later times the Persians completed the scheme for the benefit of their own country; a scheme more or less similar to the Suez canal.

The Persian invasion of Egypt occurred in the Twenty-sixth Dynasty, about 525 B.C., and the struggle of Egypt against a foreign oppressor continued. Indeed, her history through the centuries has shown that under foreign domination revolutions repeatedly occurred and neither occupied nor occupier enjoyed any quiet or constructive period, except during the six hundred years of Roman occupation.

The next illustrious name to appear in Egypt's history is that of Alexander the Great, the Macedonian who changed the course of world events. His conquests in Persia brought him to Egypt, where he was hailed as a deliverer. He became impressed with the system of kingship in the country and the philosophy of the land.

[1] There is still a strong and growing Greek community—mainly mercantile—in Alexandria.

Alexander was crowned in the Temples of Memphis and Heliopolis and given the traditional titles of the Pharaohs. After a visit to the desert oasis of Siwa, he heard the voice of God in his shrine—and then Alexander believed he was himself divine and the son of Amon.[1]

On his death-bed, he asked to be buried in Siwa near his "father" Amon—forgetting all his glories, his Macedonian birthplace; his mother Olympia, who awaited his return. Alexander's followers brought his body from Asia to Memphis, but while they were preparing to take the royal body to Siwa, his General, Ptolemy, insisted upon burying him in a great mausoleum in Alexandria.

From the time of its foundation, Alexandria became the metropolis of the ancient world; it was the seat of the ruling house of Ptolemy, who built palaces and temples, but, more than this, founded the great library and museum in which the great philosophers of Egypt and the ancient world could study, carry out investigations and teach the young amid the great wealth of ancient and contemporary books.

From thirty years before Christ, for six hundred years, Egypt was a province of the Roman Empire, subject, we may suppose, to much the same kind of rule as Britain during the Roman occupation of England.

In A.D. 640 the Moslem invasion started. The Christians in Egypt were defeated and subjugated and Egypt became a province of the Eastern Caliphate. During the whole of the sixteenth and seventeenth centuries, Egypt was incorporated as part of the Ottoman Empire and was ruled by Pashas sent by the Sultan from Constantinople. The eighteenth century saw the rule of the Mamelukes who, in the beginning, had been prisoners and slaves of the Kings of Egypt, captured in war. Mahomet Ali threw out the Mamelukes in 1905 and made himself hereditary Governor of Egypt, his position being confirmed by a "firman" from the Sultan dated June 1st, 1841.

Bonaparte conquered Egypt at the height of his power and infused strong French influence into Egyptian culture and the practice of government. But Nelson's victory in the Battle of Aboukir Bay (miscalled the Battle of the Nile) compelled Bonaparte's return to Europe—and to Waterloo.

Two events brought the British to Egypt. The Arab revolt of

[1] Rulers of Egypt, from the earliest times, have claimed divine inspiration; Alexander merely improved on this.

1882, and the rising, in the south, of Sheik Mahomat Ahmed who proclaimed himself a Mahdi of Islam.

Ahmed Arabi Pasha, revolting against a weak and corrupt Khedive, had Egypt in his power when the British arrived and were able to restore the Khedive's authority. The Mahdi's revolt led to even more serious consequences and is now part of the lives of General Gordon and Lord Kitchener.

The British army was not recalled after these revolts had been quelled, but stayed on, as an army of occupation, until 1936.

On December 18th, 1914, Britain declared a protectorate over Egypt. The Khedive was deposed. The British protectorate came to an end on February 28th, 1922, and Sultan Ahmed Fuad was proclaimed King of Egypt.

On August 26th, 1936, a treaty was signed in London, proclaiming Egypt a sovereign independent state, but British troops still held the Suez canal, and the Sudan was ruled, in theory, by an Anglo-Egyptian co-dominium, but, in fact, by a small, extremely able British Civil Service.

Egypt was invaded by Axis troops in 1940 and its safety was not secured until the Battle of Egypt in October and November, 1942, when the German and Italian forces were driven out of the country.

British troops were withdrawn from the Suez Canal bases as a result of the Heads of Agreement initialled in Cairo on July 27th, 1954;[1] while the Sudan has gained independence as a result of the Anglo-Egyptian Sudan Agreement of February 12th, 1953.

It can fairly be said that, at last, after two thousand years of domination, first by one imperial power, then by another, Egypt, at last, is free.

When, therefore, soon after the successful revolution of July 23rd, 1952, General Neguib and Colonel Nasser addressed a huge demonstration of excited Egyptians in the Square of the Revolution in Cairo, it was natural for Colonel Nasser to declare, as he did, with deep emotion:

"Lift your heads, brothers. Oppression is past. The age of freedom has arrived!"

Writing now, in the autumn of 1956, I am convinced that the Revolution in Egypt, which is now four years old, aims not only at

[1] From the 17th to the 24th of June, 1956, evacuation festivities to celebrate the final withdrawal of the last British troops from the Canal were held with great and genuine public rejoicing.

securing independence (that has now been accomplished) but at re-creating, step by step, Egyptian ascendancy in the Middle East. We are dealing with a new Empire, at present an Empire of the mind, but, in the near future perhaps, an Empire of political fact; to be achieved by the unification of the Arab peoples under the guiding crescent star of a resurgent Egypt.

To me this seems the most exciting international development of the last decade. All Anglo-American influence—as opposed to legitimate commercial interests—in the Middle East is directly challenged, and, looming ahead, is the desperate political battle for Arab oil.

CHAPTER THREE

IN THE NIGHT, SILENTLY

THE scandal of defective arms supplied to the Egyptian Army in the field in the Palestinian war, the suspicion that their King was always ready to compromise with the British, the great wealth of the royal family, and the corruption of Ministers were the main reasons for the 1952 Revolution. Yet, as late as 1950, the Army as a whole still believed that it could bring pressure on King Farouk and obtain the desired reforms under his rule.[1]

It was the crisis in the Army Officers' Club that sparked the swift, silent Revolution of July 23rd, 1953.

Matters came to a head when the time came for the election of the Executive Board of the club. The King insisted upon the nomination of Hussein Sirry Amer, officer commanding the Frontiers Administration, as Chairman of the Board, but the group of young officers who called themselves the Free Officers' Movement objected most strenuously to the King's candidate. One of the most popular of the young officers was a Lieutenant Abdel Kader Taha. At a meeting of the Officers' Club, attended by hundreds of officers to discuss the problem presented by the King's demand, news was received that Lieutenant Abdel Kader Taha had been murdered. Though there was no evidence that the young man had met his death as a result of a royal conspiracy, the Free Officers believed that the Palace had had a hand in the matter. All the officers present, three hundred and fifty-five in number, rose, and stood in silence as a sign of mourning and respect for the dead man.

There is no doubt that the Free Officers now felt that it was a question of now or never. They felt themselves marked, and openly menaced by the Palace. They decided to strike while they still had

[1] The Wafd had been agitating for democratic reform and release from foreign domination throughout the reign of King Farouk. Unfortunately, under Mehas Pasha, the party had been diverted from its true aims.

the capacity to do so. There were only six in the original group, headed by Nasser. Soon others joined, but the utmost care had to be taken. It was realized that the Palace, which had vast funds at its disposal for uncovering treason, would try to penetrate the secret meetings of the Free Officers, if possible obtaining a tape recording of their conversations. This would be produced at the subsequent trials, and long periods of imprisonment or death awaited the trapped men. So, cautiously, one by one, they increased their numbers.

In a secret leaflet issued at the time by the Free Officers, it was stated that, for two months, a wave of terror had swept over the country, personal liberty had disappeared, free press organs had been suppressed and about 5,000 patriots had been locked up in jails and internment camps for no other offence than taking part in the national struggle.

The leaflet further stressed the fact that even army officers had fallen victims to this régime of terror.

The Free Officers realized that the movement was no longer confined to camps and barracks, but involved popular elements, and that some drastic action should be taken at the earliest opportunity.

The Government faced them with an order, closing down the Officers' Club and dissolving its Executive Board; and the then Minister of the Interior, in anticipation of increased popular resistance, provided the police with armoured cars to quell any popular rising supported by the Army.

In another circular, the Free Officers warned their colleagues against the obvious trend to use the armed forces for the suppression of any insurrection.

The Hussein Sirry[1] Government came into power at a time when the King insisted upon the appointment of Hussein Sirry Amer, a pro-Palace General, as Minister of War and Marine.

Hussein Sirry resigned and Hilaly was again entrusted with the task of forming a new Government. He chose as War Minister Ismail Sherin, a brother-in-law of the former King, who had never been to any military academy. Matters became aggravated and the

[1] Although Hussein Sirry was not a professional soldier, he was well liked, personally, by the Army. Highly educated and charming, he married the King's sister, the former Queen of Iran; and had been Head of the Palestine Department of the Ministry of War.

political atmosphere was overcast. The Free Officers remained sleepless for two nights, debating the drastic step to be taken.

Their faith in the people was such that they decided to take immediate action.

On the night of July 22nd, they started the execution of one of the most daring military coups in history.

By the early morning of July 23rd, the movement had been successfully carried into effect.

Nasser is a born revolutionary. The literature that most attracts him is the history of the technique of the *coup d'état.* His knowledge stood him in good stead in the early hours of the morning of the 23rd.

Two factors are important in all such enterprises. The conspirators must be able to give the effective orders. The rebels must be able to seize at once the key positions of their operation. Nasser was helped by the centralization of Government in Egypt. It was necessary, above all, to surround the King and his ministers so that they could give no counter orders. This was done, swiftly, silently. It was essential for the rebels to seize the Ministry of Defence, the postal services and the Radio station. At 9 a.m. they were able to broadcast a *fait accompli* to the nation. "The Army, on behalf of the people, has taken over."

Even so, in the interregnum before the King left on the 26th, the people remained passive, hoping that the Army would succeed without bloodshed. After the King's departure, it was realized that the revolutionaries had, indeed, triumphed. There was an upsurge of popular feeling in favour of the revolt. Nasser and his comrades felt themselves, for the first time, secure.

The seizure of the key points was only possible because the few Free Officers were just the right men to give the orders necessary. The highest ranks, the Generals and Brigadiers, were too far removed from direct executive orders to garrisons. They were not brought into the plot. Nor were the junior officers and non-commissioned ranks told of what was afoot. They were too low on the ladder to realize the significance of orders received. Even if they did so, they would not disobey their Colonel. So the Colonels and the Majors carried the day. The troops themselves, during the fatal night, had no knowledge of what they were doing. Unusual orders to occupy public buildings were not unknown in Cairo when a Government changed or street rioting was feared. The simple soldiers of Egypt did what they were told. Later they realized that they had taken part in the first great Egyptian revolution since Oraby had seized the city and come to terms with the frightened Khedive, Tewfik, in 1881.

Remote country garrisons and civil administrations were taken by telephone. The new Government merely sent a message that they were now in power, and that strict obedience to all future instructions would be insisted on, any disobedience most severely dealt with. Nasser sent carefully worded messages to the British and American Embassies stating that foreign rights and property would be respected.

At this critical moment, the revolutionaries feared only one development. They thought it possible that British troops stationed at the Canal base might come to the King's aid. Farouk was a General in the British Army, the relationship between Whitehall and the Egyptian Crown had at times been close. But the British Government at that time had no liking for the King, whom they thought had let down monarchical prestige. No British aid was forthcoming. The Foreign Office issued a statement saying that the Egyptian revolution was purely "an internal affair". How wrong they were to prove, experience in the Near and Far East should have warned them. Apart from political considerations, the public in Britain and America welcomed the new régime. The British Prime Minister, in particular, extended a welcoming hand to General Neguib and Colonel Nasser.

The sequence of events during the fateful night of July 22nd-23rd and throughout the 23rd and the following days has a drama all its own.

At 7 a.m. on Wednesday July 23rd, 1952, a radio broadcast announced to Egypt and to the world that the Army had assumed authority to eliminate corruption and put an end to anarchy and despotism. It further pointed out that corrupt cliques had caused the Army's ordeal in Palestine.

It was, therefore, deemed imperative, it continued, that some drastic action should be taken by the Army, who would ensure the country's welfare.

The statement was welcomed by millions who rejoiced in the feeling that at long last something had been done to eliminate a state of things which had brought shame on the country and had caused untold suffering to the people. The people realized that, for the first time during seventy years, complete freedom had been secured.

As for King Farouk, he apparently had not listened to the broadcast. When Dr. Hafez Afifi, the Chief of the Royal Cabinet, tried to get in touch with him by 'phone at the Montazah Palace to receive his instructions as to the action to be taken, Mohammed Hassan,[1] the King's valet, replied by asking him to communicate to him the message which he would convey to his royal master.

However, panic soon reigned in the palace and the "responsible" authorities were perplexed and frightened. They were informed in the most categorical terms that any intrigue by them to invoke foreign aid would be sternly and immediately dealt with.

At 3 p.m. the same day, former Premier Naguib El Hilaly, feeling that he was not in a position to cope with the situation, decided to tender his resignation, which was immediately accepted.

The King, accustomed to deal with such politicians as were easily bribed into an attitude, if not of open acquiescence, at any rate of passive submission, found, to his cost, that he was faced with a different type of man—young officers who had risked their lives to deliver their country from a state of material chaos and moral rottenness.

Even at the time when Sayed Aly Maher was entrusted by royal decree with the task of forming a new government, the palace circles believed that the Army would be satisfied if certain corrupt elements in the royal entourage were excluded and a number of its grievances redressed.

Wishful thinking led these circles further to believe that the movement had not won the unqualified support of the Army or the people.

A number of members of the royal household were dismissed, not without some reluctance on the part of the man who still sat on the throne, but such measures could not possibly satisfy the Revolution leaders, who were convinced of the absolute necessity of getting rid of Farouk.

On July 26th, Army contingents surrounded the royal palaces in Alexandria. Farouk drove from Montazah to the Ras El Tine Palace, in the hope that his bodyguard might defend him.

At 9 a.m. the Army addressed its historic ultimatum to the King

[1] Mohammed Hassan was the Nubian valet of King Farouk. He had far too much authority, and, on one occasion, even State documents in his possession.

asking him to abdicate by noon and to leave the country by 6 a.m. the same day.

Premier Aly Maher motored at once to the Ras El Tine Palace, where he had to pass through a cordon of tanks, armoured cars and infantry in field kit, before he gained access to Farouk, who was virtually a prisoner in his own palace.

King Farouk, who was perplexed at the grave and unexpected turn events had taken, discovered that he was being dethroned by the people of Egypt.

At that moment, he must have recalled a similar situation when he had been threatened with the loss of his throne following an ultimatum handed to him ten years before, by a foreign ambassador whose country's tanks had encircled the Abdin Palace, one of them actually breaking through the outer fence. At that time, however, Farouk had represented in large measure the spirit of Egypt's resistance. He had been applauded by his people as a national hero.

To-day, however, it was the people, represented by the Army, who were driving him out of the country. When he learned that support was not available, he finally gave in and at 6 p.m. he left Egypt for good, accompanied by Queen Narriman, in his yacht *Fakhr el Behar*, "The Pride of the Sea".

The actual document, presented to the King, demanding his abdication, was as follows. The anger of the ultimatum contrasts strangely with His Majesty's short reply:

"Text of the Ultimatum Addressed by El Ferik Mohamed Naguib to His Majesty King Farouk In the Name of the Officers and Men of the Egyptian Armed Forces.

Cairo, July 26th, 1952.

"To His Majesty King Farouk I,

"In view of the complete Anarchy which reigned throughout the country as a result of your misdeeds, tampering with the Constitution and complete disregard of the people's will to the extent that no individual is reassured about his life, property or dignity and that Egypt's reputation among nations has considerably worsened in consequence of your continued conduct, the result has been that traitors and corrupt persons have secured, through your

Gift to his former Majesty King Farouk from the Syrian Army

Gamel Abdel Nasser

protection, security and extreme wealth and great extravagance at the expense of the poor and hungry people.

"This has been clearly demonstrated during the Palestine War and its attendant scandals about obsolete arms, as a result of which trials took place, in which you openly intervened for the distortion of the truth and for the shaking of confidence in the judicature. This conduct has encouraged traitors to follow in your footsteps, amassing enormous wealth and becoming absolutely reckless in their corrupt acts because it is said that people usually follow the example of their rulers.

"For these reasons, I have been authorized by the Army, representing the people, to ask you to abdicate in favour of your Crown Prince, Emir Ahmed Fouad, within a delay ending at noon and to leave the country by 6 p.m. to-day, the Army holding you responsible for whatever consequence may take place, following your disregard of the people's will."

The King replied in these words:

"Royal Rescript No. 65 in the Year 1952.

"We, Farouk I, King of Egypt and the Sudan,

"Whereas we always seek the welfare of our people and cherish its happiness and progress,

"Whereas we earnestly desire to make the country avoid difficulties which it is facing at this crucial juncture and in conformity with the people's will,

"We have decided to abdicate our Throne in favour of our Crown Prince, Emir Ahmed Fouad, issuing This our Rescript to His Excellency Aly Maher Pasha, President of the Council of Ministers for the necessary action.

"(Signed): FAROUK.

"Done at the Ras El-Tin Palace, July 26th, 1952."

There is no doubt that King Farouk, when the crisis came, behaved with much wisdom. Throughout the ordeal of the three days when he was surrounded and a virtual prisoner, he showed no sign of fear. His example prevented a panic in the palace. His political advisers soon deserted him, but his family were faithful, and his personal servants did not desert him. The suddenness of his departure made it necessary to leave behind an immense fortune in money as well as in precious stones, stamps and *objets d'art*. These were later auctioned. Queen Narriman was able to take her personal jewellery and the family packed some fifty cases of precious personal belongings. King Farouk had considerable investments abroad and was financially independent wherever he went. A faithful butler had managed to load on to the yacht the cream of the King's cellar: champagnes, clarets and burgundies, with a large supply of brandy and port. He could not bear, he said, to see these fall into the hands of persons who might not appreciate them. The King smiled for the first time since the revolution had broken, when he heard this.[1]

King Farouk had formed the astute impression that he owed his escape to the underlying loyalty of General Neguib and the older Army officers, who had managed up to the last moment to keep the young, hot-headed Free Officers group at a distance from their sovereign. The King suspected that, the moment he left Egyptian soil, the young officers would no longer tolerate any restraint. He thought that, regretting his escape and fearing his return, they might even send a frigate to pursue him and order his return. In that event he believed that death awaited him in Egypt. So, that evening, the *Fakhr el Bihar* steamed north-west as though heading for France, but, during the night, she altered course and made for Italy. During her silent steaming through the night, no navigation lights were shown, nor was any radio communication used. The King was taking no chances.

Farouk's abdication, however, did not put an end to monarchy. Infant Prince Ahmed Fuad was proclaimed King and a Regency Council was constituted. It was quite clear, however, that the majority of the people demanded the abolition of monarchy and the establishment of a republic.

An informal but significant referendum undertaken by a weekly review indicated an unmistakable popular trend towards the abolition of monarchy.

It was decided at the same time that some Revolution Command

[1] King Farouk was accorded full honours for his departure. It was Egypt exiling its King. Ali Mayer was there. So was General Neguib. The only member of the Diplomatic Corps present was the American Ambassador. The British representative was, unfortunately, absent.

officers should hold ministerial portfolios, Lt.-Colonel Gamal Abdel Nasser becoming Deputy Premier and Minister for the Interior; Wing Commander Abdel Latif Boghdadi, Minister of War and Marine; Major Salah Salem, Minister of National Guidance and Minister of State for Sudan Affairs; and Major-General Abdel Hakim Amer, Commander-in-Chief of the Egyptian Armed Forces.

As soon as the King had sailed, the new leaders started to reorganize Egypt. Two major problems had to be tackled: the Constitution and the monarchy.

A declaration issued on February 10th, 1953, by the Prime Minister, General Mohamed Neguib, in his capacity as Commander-in-Chief of the Armed Forces and Leader of the Army Revolution, defined the constitutional system of government under which the country would be ruled during the three-year transition period.

Under this important constitutional declaration, which was issued by General Neguib in the name of the people, acts of supreme sovereignty, particularly the adoption of measures to protect the Revolution, the system on which it is based and the right to appoint and dismiss Cabinet Ministers are vested in the Leader of the Revolution sitting in Council of the Revolution Command.

The text of the declaration consists of two sections—the first on general principles and the second on the system of government of eleven articles.

The preamble explains that the declaration emanated from "the desire to stabilize the system of Government during the transition period, define the rights and duties of all citizens, and enable the country to enjoy complete tranquillity which would make for fruitful production and the raising of the country's standard to the level desired by all, possible."

In making the declaration, the Leader of the Revolution renewed his unshakable faith in the necessity for creating a democratic constitutional system of government following the transition period and ensuring a free life and a better future for all.

The declaration vests the executive and legislative powers in the Council of Ministers, while Ministers assume executive powers in respect to their particular Ministries.

It affirms the independence of the judiciary and says that judgments would be pronounced "in the name of the people".

The functions of the Congress will be to discuss general policy of the State and related matters as well as to question Cabinet Ministers on their ministerial acts.

The declaration guarantees freedom of belief, thought, individual freedom, the sanctity of homes and property within the provisions of the law.

It asserts that the people are the source of all authority and all Egyptians are equal before the law in regard to their rights and duties. Under the declaration, the extradition of political refugees is forbidden. It further lays down that no taxes or fees can be levied except by law.

The provisional constitution, in fact, retained all ultimate power in the hands of the Revolutionary Council during the interim three-year period. Military courts were set up to try political offenders, and the machinery of a military dictatorship set in motion.

The time for political parties, full enfranchisement and elections had not yet come.

Nasser was dissatisfied with the monarchical position. The baby Crown Prince Ahmed Fuad was with his father, Farouk, which gave the parent some power. Besides, there would have to be a regency during the Crown Prince's minority, and this might pave the way for a future full-scale return to power for the Crown. This Nasser was determined to prevent.

The Revolution Council, therefore, issued the following statement at midnight on June 18th, 1953:

"The Revolution was brought about in order to put an end to imperialism and its partisans. On July 26th, 1952, ex-King Farouk was asked to abdicate his throne as he represented the corner-stone on which imperialism depended.

"However, since that date and since the abolition of parties, certain elements with outmoded ideas have leaned for their existence and survival upon the monarchial régime which the whole nation was unanimous in wishing to see disappear for ever.

"The history of the Mohamed Aly family in Egypt has been a series of acts of treason to the prejudice of the people. One of the first of these treasons was incontestably the pleasures in which Ismail drowned himself, drowning the country with him in the debts which destroyed his reputation as well as his finances. Moreover, this gave a pretext for the imperialist nations to infiltrate into this country.

"Then came Tewfik to complete this phase of open treason in order to safeguard his throne. The armies of occupation penetrated into Egypt to protect the foreigner seated on the throne, who demanded aid against his own people from the enemies of his country. It was as a result of this attitude that imperialism and the throne were associated for their mutual profit. The one gave power to the other in their mutual interest.

"Each party thus reduced the people to slavery in the name of the other; and the throne became the screen behind which imperialism acted in order to drain away the people's food and destroy its structure, efforts and liberties.

"Farouk surpassed his predecessors. He enriched and perjured himself. He became a despot without conscience thus tracing with his own hands his end and his destiny.

"The moment has, therefore, come for the country to free itself from every trace of the servitude imposed on it by these events.

"We, therefore, proclaim to-day in the name of the people the abolition of the monarchy, the end of the dynasty of Mohamed Aly as well as that of the titles of the members of that family.

"We proclaim the Republic. Major-General Mohamed Neguib, Chief of the Revolution, becomes President of the Republic at the same time conserving his present powers under the provisional constitution. This Government will remain in power during the whole transitional period and the people will have the last word on the form of the Republic and the choice of the President with the promulgation of the new Constitution.

"Let us have faith in God and in ourselves. May God help us and grant us success!"

Success was not denied the leaders of the Egyptian Revolution. As soon as it was realized that Britain and America, by taking no action, had assented to the change in régime, fifty other Governments, in rapid succession, recognized the Neguib-Nasser régime. An intensive press campaign against the former King was started in Cairo and the foreign correspondents caught the general trend and wired hostile comments on Farouk to their head offices. The King was accused of every ignominy. He made no reply. Twice in his life he had caught the imagination of the Egyptian people; first, as a young man, returning from Britain, handsome and pleasing, he had seemed to be Allah's envoy. Then during the war, when

British tanks had surrounded the Abdin Palace and virtually arrested the King, forcing him to change Prime Ministers,[1] he had seemed to be the champion of Egyptian national aspirations. These memories he took with him when he sailed to exile and to silence.

The constitution of 1923 had never worked. The King had had to take a leading part in the stormy sea of Egyptian politics, playing off the ambitions of one party against another. The charge that his conduct was treasonable, that he constantly connived at British domination, is without foundation. When the passions and prejudices of the present are past, history will pronounce its judgment on King Farouk and on the Mahomet Aly dynasty.

Meanwhile, the restless, ambitious Colonel Nasser took over and started to drive Egypt towards her new destiny as a free nation and the spearhead of an Arab renaissance. The repercussions of this "purely internal affair" were to reach out over the Near East and profoundly affect the chances of world peace and the interests of Britain and America and France. In modern guise Mahomet had returned to scourge the infidel.

[1] Mustafa El Naha was the British nominee.

NOTE. There has been much speculation as to when and how King Farouk lost his hold on the loyalty and affection of his people.

Most observers say that the turning point was his divorce from Queen Farida. He had three daughters by the Queen, but no son. Their differences, however, did not concern the succession, but the King's personal behaviour.

The Queen objected to the King's private life and to his immediate entourage. She objected, even more strongly, to the small coterie round the King, especially to Mohammed Hassan, the Nubian valet, and to Karen Thabet, a personal friend of the King's, who had been given an official post at Court as "Press Adviser".

A senior member of the family attempted a reconciliation between the King and Queen, but nothing came of it.

CHAPTER FOUR

GAMAL ABDEL NASSER

SINCE the swift, bloodless revolution of July 23rd, 1952, which made Gamel Abdel Nasser master of Egypt, a picture of Nasser has been built up in Britain and America: a picture which the facts seemed to justify. This man, with the dominating nose and boundless energy, has been presented as dangerously ambitious and as nursing a deep, damaging hatred of the West, and all that it stands for. In Cairo I was given unusual opportunities for finding out the real truth about Nasser. Now I think I know what makes Nasser scheme. I also think I know what goes on in the Nasser mind, apart from politics.

He is unusually tall for an Egyptian. Six feet, the papers say, but, in fact, five feet eleven and a half. The arrogant, dictatorial nose is there, certainly. It is the most remarkable, but not the most significant, feature of his face. For this handsome man of thirty-seven has the eyes of a visionary, of a prophet, but of a prophet very much in touch with this world, as well as with his dreams. The eyes express the force and speed of his thought. One can see his thoughts, sharp and rapid, reflected in them. He has a latent hypnotic power. Of all the V.I.P.s from Britain who have interviewed him, only one came away with an adverse verdict. The rest surrendered unconditionally.

The fact is that Colonel Nasser, as well as courage and industry, has charm. He exercises it without any conscious effort. A distinguished soldier who had been in conference with him for hours on end, said: "I could almost feel the man's attraction. It seemed to emanate from him as something tangible and fill the room as a physical force. It is extraordinarily difficult to disagree with what he says."

With this all-important quality of personal magnetism Nasser must have been born. His rise to fame is a fantastic story. His father was a small official in the postal service but the family were cultivators at Beini Morr, a tiny Egyptian hamlet. The handsome, restless youth wanted, at first, to be a lawyer, in common with hundreds of other ambitious young Egyptians, but vacancies occurred for cadets in the rapidly expanding Egyptian Army and he decided to fashion his career as a soldier.

Courage is the hall-mark of a soldier, just as piety is that of a priest. Young Nasser had abounding courage. As a youth, he forced his way to the front of any group of marching, nationalist students. On two occasions companions were killed or wounded. Nasser was not touched. In the Palestine war, a cynical and perverted public opinion in Cairo was forced to admit that this man was unique. The press called him "The Tiger of Faluja" and the name stuck.[1] Since he has come to power, only one of the three attempts on his life has had any publicity: the desperate assassination attempt in November 1954, by Abdel Latif, when seven shots were fired, wounding a minister standing next to Nasser. Even in the moment of pandemonium, Nasser could control himself and the terrified crowd. "Sit down! Sit down! Arrest that man." Then he added, with a sincerity that none could doubt, as the crowd listened in awed silence: "I am ready to die for Egypt any day. You all know that."

When seeking the key to Nasser's character, I gradually unravelled the pattern of this man's life, his background, habits and dreams. He was married very young, in the manner of many Moslems, and is still married to the same good woman who has given him five children—two are boys—and unswerving devotion in the home, where, she thinks, her kingdom is.

Colonel Nasser seems to have a natural love of simplicity. The only chattel of grandeur near him in his office is a gold ink-stand, the gift of an Arab chief. It is exquisitely worked and is at least a more civilized product than the macabre ink-well presented to Queen Victoria made from the Mahdi's skull.

His whole enormous energy is poured, day after day, and night after night, into the two ambitions he has taken as his guiding stars. The first is to rid the Middle East, and Egypt in particular, of Western domination, and the second is like unto it: to unite the rich,

[1] Although Colonel Nasser won fame in the Palestinian war, he was virtually unknown to the Egyptian public until after the removal of General Neguib, the first public revolutionary leader; but Colonel Nasser led the Revolution from the wings and largely conceived it.

oil-producing Arab-speaking nations in a great Arab Commonwealth which would, he thinks, secure the peace and progress of the Arab world.

These, apart from the High Dam and its finance from Suez Canal revenues, are his great public ambitions, but Nasser has his intimate, intensely human side as well. He has no trace of pomposity. His favourite drink: tea. His favourite game: chess. Both are linked with his faith and character. The Moslems can take no alcohol. The scheming brain of the man finds relaxation in chess. "Just like life," he says of the game. Not, perhaps, like your life or mine, but very like his.

Is he irrevocably anti-British, nursing a deep hatred of this country? Consider two minor, but significant actions.

At the height of Anglo-Egyptian tension and distrust, he employed Mr. Williams-Thompson, a director of the City public relations firm of Sidney Barton Ltd., as Government spokesman to handle his international contacts.

Then, while he was being pictured as a ruthless dictator, he heard, in April last year, the story of the English schoolboy, Howard Jones, who was so fascinated by Egyptology that he sold a private museum for five pounds and, taking an autocycle, tried to reach Egypt by way of Spain. When Nasser read this, he dropped some important and complicated work he was grappling with, and, turning to his secretary, said: "We must get that boy here. I wanted to do things like that when I was a lad. I never could. See that he is invited here."

The secretary was surprised but the wheels were set in motion. The grave Egyptian Ambassador in London, Abdul Rahman Hakki, read, incredulously, his instructions: "Find Howard Jones. Invite him here." Great was the activity at the Embassy in South Audley Street. Where is Kenton? And where, oh where, is Elmwood Avenue, the home of Howard Jones' parents?

All the difficulties were ironed out. The boy and his mother were flown to Egypt where the "young professor" was treated with much kindness and given a carved Pharaoh and pottery from a newly opened tomb. The boy's dream had come true. And one dream of Abdel Gamal Nasser had come true. When they met, the tall, smiling soldier and the neat English schoolboy, they seemed to find common ground immediately. A friend of Nasser said: "His heart was touched. I have never seen him more gentle. The acceptance of his invitation by this English schoolboy had, for some reason made him very happy."

What was the reason? Could it have been that the young Howard Jones, happy, interested and grateful, was a better ambassador than all the professionals put together?

My studies of the Egyptian scene convinced me, in the end, that Nasser personally has respect for Britain. He has hatred, yes, but it is for something he dreads and fears. He hates the idea of British domination over his own country. He resents, fanatically, the assumption that the Middle East is still, in fact, a British sphere of influence, and, on the personal side, the cool, impeccable, slightly supercilious manners of some British diplomats and servicemen rile him unbearably. An inferiority complex? I think not. Most Egyptians, because of their faith and ancient civilization, are apt to regard themselves as innately superior to Europeans and Asians.

For over five thousand years, the Egyptians have enjoyed real civilization: not the refrigerator, washing-machine conveniences, but art, culture, a way of life and thought that were unrivalled in their complexity and depth. Yet, they seldom had freedom. The Persians, the Greeks, the Arabs, the Turks conquered Egypt.[1] Then quite recently, opening up a new Western world, came the French and British. Even the rulers were foreigners. King Farouk speaks much better French than he does Arabic. Now, at last, Egypt is free, completely free. It is a wonderful, intoxicating change. It has intoxicated Nasser and his fellow-officers to this extent: they want always to do the "free-est" thing they can. And, as we were the last rulers of Egypt, they often take action that makes the British Foreign Office jump in agitation.

From his reaction, Nasser's public acts derive. Quite recently, he admitted this. "I don't have a foreign policy. I merely react to what Britain does." He will award a commercial contract to the Russians if their bid is the best. "Why not?" he will say. "Who is going to stop us?" The answer is, of course, no one. The Soviet dancers are welcome in Cairo. "Why not? They dance very well and we like their performance." Egyptian officers are sent to Russia for training. "Why must we always send them to Sandhurst or West Point? That would give you a monopoly."

[1] It must be admitted that the Egyptians tended to assimilate their conquerors rather than the reverse. French manners and customs permeated only the upper class, as they did throughout Europe.

This waving of the freedom flag does not mean that Nasser is a Communist or a dictator, though he is much nearer to being a dictator than he likes to admit. He says: "No, I don't think I can fairly be called a dictator. I am a sentimentalist." When he is charged with Communist sympathies, largely on account of his vast land reform programme, he laughs. "You don't know the Egyptians if you say that. We are incurably individualistic. One of my basic difficulties is that, as yet, there is no informed, unified public opinion in Cairo or in the country. It is not easy to lead a nation that has no mind of its own. But we are improving. Now that we are no longer dominated, a more stable, national feeling is emerging; and this feeling—patriotism if you like—is linked with the feelings of our brother Arabs in Jordan, Syria, Saudi Arabia and the other Arab States."

As he speaks on this theme, the restless, dominating vision of the man is at its height. The Egyptians call their link with other Arab States the Arab League, but the real vision seems to be an Arab Commonwealth. We should never underestimate this side of Nasser's ambition, for it has a very solid foundation. There are only twenty-three million Egyptians, and they depend, financially, on their cotton crop, which is in decreasing demand, but in the Near East there are ten Arab States with a population of eighty millions and a great wealth from oil. If Nasser's dream comes true—and his dreams often do—he would be the political leader of a new force in world affairs, of a rich, powerful Middle Eastern Arab world with the closest ties, religious, commercial, strategic and linguistic. Moreover, Egypt's economic problem, an expanding population in a contracting world cotton market, would not be insuperable, as now it sometimes appears to be.

There is no doubt that, though Nasser has pressed on hard with his land reforms, with the vast High Dam project, and with a score of other development schemes at home, his heart is set on the Arab Commonwealth dream. Nasser believes that Britain intends to thwart his ambition by the Baghdad pact and by using the wealth of Middle Eastern oil for her own purposes and those of her allies. At present he cannot be shaken out of this conviction, though he knows that the British Foreign Office is reviewing its Near Eastern policy, hesitating whether it should try to defeat Nasser as an enemy or win him as a friend.[1] His absorption with the idea of Arab unity led

[1] The Suez Canal Company nationalization ended this hesitancy.

to one of the most dramatic moments in his career, and to a chilling experience for Mr. Selwyn Lloyd.

The scene is Cairo. There had been political discussions during the day, Nasser sticking boldly to his points. "This is our area. It's Arab, not American, or British, or French. Yes, you have your oil interests. All right, go ahead, work your oil, but don't interfere with us. Don't try to preserve your spheres of influence. Face the facts. We're free. Absolutely free—and we mean to go our own way."

Reasonably, understandingly, the British Foreign Secretary had replied: "Your Excellency is free. Egypt is free. But the peace and security of the Middle East concerns the world, not only the Arab nations. Our pact is not directed against you. Without it you would be vulnerable."

It had been a long day of tortuous argument, a tiring day. At the end, only Nasser seemed as fresh, as virile as ever. The Foreign Secretary was glad to relax at dinner, an excellent dinner, in the ornate Tehra Palace. Colonel Nasser was charming, the attentive host, the delightful raconteur. He listened as well as he spoke. Mr. Selwyn Lloyd congratulated Nasser on the brandy as they sat after dinner with their coffee, that thick, sweet Egyptian coffee that makes our British coffee seem a pale shadow. For a moment, there was silence in the room. Conversation, as will happen even when Prime Ministers and Foreign Secretaries are present—or could it be because they are present?—had languished.

Colonel Nasser leaned forward and his words, spoken in little more than a whisper, struck the Foreign Secretary with a cruel impact.

"Does your Excellency know that King Hussein has just dismissed General Glubb?"

Mr. Selwyn Lloyd did not know. Nor did he know what to say. He was able to keep outwardly calm, making an ineffective, but polite rejoinder.

We cannot doubt that that night Gamal Abdel Nasser went happily to bed.

We may blame Nasser for his dramatic gestures, but we must admit that he would be hardly human if he did not induge in them, now that power has come his way. For eighty years we have had a large well-equipped Army on Egyptian soil, an Army that could have taken Cairo in a day. During the war, rightly and under duress, we did not hesitate to dictate to the Egyptian King and government. All that time Egyptians were always in a position of being told what had happened, of plans others had conceived, of decisions others had made. They never had anything of their own to hide, or to surprise the world with.

So now Nasser hides with relish his jet aircraft and his latest weapons in the Sinai desert, where the Israelis cannot find them or seize them, as they might do if there were a real clash and they were moved into the Gaza strip. When, in February 1955, the Israeli forces showed their strength by cutting the Gaza strip in two and then withdrawing, it was a shock to Nasser. He has concentrated on collecting new weapons ever since.

The bomb he exploded so deftly in front of Mr. Selwyn Lloyd was prompted by the same spirit. Glubb Pasha stood for all that Nasser hates: an accepted, irremovable, British imperialism. When he comes up against any aspect of imperialism, Nasser is not as balanced or as shrewd as he usually is. "Imperialism," he said recently, "is like a bad woman who will always give in when she is faced by force." I don't think he quite believes this, but he would like to. It is the same with the United Nations.

No major statesman has said as often as Nasser has: "I don't believe in the United Nations." What he really means is that, in Arab eyes, the United Nations means Britain and America, and more Britain than America. Egyptian politicians have long held the flattering, but odd view, that what Britain plans to-day the United States will do tomorrow. Yet, when the Secretary-General of the United Nations visited Cairo recently, to attempt an Israeli-Egyptian settlement, Colonel Nasser treated him with much consideration, and was far less defiant and unhelpful than he has ever been with British and American visiting statesmen.

It has been suggested that Nasser's constant activity in foreign affairs is deliberate in order to hide the slowness of the Egyptian Revolution at home. This is completely false. In the first three years this dynamic overriding personality has forced through more reforms than the Mahomet Aly Dynasty had introduced in 150 years. In a country where eighty-five per cent of the rural population were landless and 1,500 landowners owned most of the small area of richly cultivated Nile Valley land, he introduced, and pressed on with, his small-holding policy, using the great forfeited estates of the ruling house to initiate his schemes.

He moved the vast High Dam project, costing over four hundred millions, from blue print to active planning and contracting. He linked to it the great nitrate fertilizer plant to be worked by the High Dam power. A twenty million pound iron and steel works is to be constructed by a German firm. Russian, American, British, French and German firms are competing for twenty other major projects including irrigation, great Nile bridges and munition factories.

Nasser has only been able to do this because his personal habits are unique in allowing him about fifteen working hours a day.

The Nasser idea of a well-proportioned day would not suit everybody, but, apparently, it suits him. His doctor, whom he consults, but does not obey, says he is in perfect condition.

He divides the twenty-four hours into fifteen hours of work, with one or two breaks for meals and outside engagements, and nine hours for sleep and for recreation with his family. He starts work around nine in the morning (Egyptian officials have, reluctantly, to follow suit) and works until midnight. There are two breaks for meals and the day is peppered with interviews, meetings, parades and other diversions. Nevertheless, it is an Homeric schedule. That leaves him from midnight until nine next day at home. He still lives in the modest, suburban house he occupied as a Colonel without any other rank. He rises at six. On waking, as a good Moslem he takes his praying mat and, facing Mecca and the breaking dawn of an Eastern heaven, prays alone and undisturbed. The whole early morning, including school-leaving time for the junior Nassers, is spent at home. He says six hours' sleep is his quota. If he sleeps longer, he gets " bored ".

His mind, until recently, was very much occupied, apart from his foreign political plans, with operating the Constitution: on paper, a liberal and progressive one, with a singe-elected assembly and a President. Both the Constitution and the Presidential office are to be made the subject of a plebiscite, but the odds on Nasser being chosen President are short. He is, in fact, a certainty for that post.[1]

The constitutional issue he regards as a great gamble. Nasser's idea is that, as he gives land to the landless fellaheen, he will build up a great body of popular support among the masses. At present he is playing safe. The Political Parties' Law has not yet been promulgated; and the first members of the Assembly are to be nominated. By whom? By Colonel Nasser and his advisers. It is easy

[1] Forecast confirmed by events!

to ridicule this political situation, but, in fairness, no other course seems open to him. The supreme test for Nasser will come later, with the constitution working and political parties, pro- and anti-government, operating. We shall then see whether he is able to bring about the promised freedom of the press (at present heavily censored) and freedom of speech. Religious freedom is not a problem. It has existed in Egypt in modern times. The large body of Christian, as well as the Jews, carry on their faiths without molestation, while Islam remains the State religion. The Presidential Law provides for the office to be held for six years. That gives Nasser time to win or lose Egypt. If, within that period, he contrives to turn himself into a popular Egyptian leader, backed by a majority vote, history will account him a great man. If, at each threat or adverse trend, he is tempted to roll out the tanks, or seek the turbulent refuge of war, he will be just another Army officer who has seized power from a weak and corrupt régime.

At present his popularity with the poeple is undoubted. He is St. George to the Egyptian crowd. The dragon? Britain and the western "imperialists". This does not mean that the Egyptians hate either America or Britain. We are portrayed as the Big Brother who is always interfering; Nasser as the champion standing up for Egyptian rights. The hatred is reserved for Israel, and it is pathetically vicious and stubborn. The very word "Israel" is printed on certain official documents with the capital "I" in the shape of a dagger dripping blood. Nasser will work patiently, for years if necessary, to achieve his Arab unity, and, at the propitious moment, he and his allies will try to wipe out the new Israeli State. If the Secretary-General of UNO or President Eisenhower think otherwise, they are grievously mistaken. There is no longer an "if" in Nasser's mind. Only a "when" and a "how".

Nasser's interests are diverse, his intelligence keen. He reads voraciously. In a recent interview, he was questioned about the momentous events that had brought him into power—the corruption of King Farouk's ministers, the election dispute in the Army Officers' Club and the evil scandal of the faulty arms supplied to the Egyptian forces in the Palestinian war. Nasser showed that he had studied revolutionary technique for years. "Preparation, secrecy, swiftness. Those are the keys to success." And he went on to display an intimate knowledge of both the French and Russian Revolutions. He is versed, too, in the history of Egypt, with its recurring drama of great personalities from Imotep to Napoleon Bonaparte and Nelson. Yet I feel that both his reading and his grasp are limited. His vision is Near Eastern, not global. His prejudices are almost parochial.

Egyptians are still extraordinarily sensitive and Nasser is as sensitive as any. I cannot blame them. Only recently, in Cairo at a garden party, I was sitting next to a young British Army officer and his bride. He suggested that they should " circulate " and started to move towards a party of Egyptian officers standing close by. The girl said in that high, penetrating whisper we all know so well: " Oh, darling, no. Need we go and talk to *them*? " The tone was so casually insulting that it sent a chill down my spine.

Just over 150 years ago, after a naval engagement off Alexandria, British sailors rescued a man from the sea. He was an Albanian soldier, penniless, half-alive. He founded the Mahomet Aly Dynasty which Nasser has now destroyed. Can Nasser build a better Egypt than the Kings did? Time alone will tell.

In Cairo now, this new Saladin works feverishly to make his dreams come true. Probably, at this moment, he is in conference, arguing with some Western diplomat, his fine head, with the thick, black hair slightly greying, resting on his left hand, his dark eyes flashing their message of defiance, his words expressing his faith and his hopes.

" Why must you interfere? This is our country. The Near East is Arab. Can't you understand that? We have come into our own again. We will build our own future, shape our own destiny."

Friend or foe, here is a man to reckon with, a man who means to play a great role in the grand manner. Before I had been a week in Cairo, I realized that Nasser was that strange mixture of determination, intuitive vision and deep conviction which combine to make a political leader of the calibre of Kemal Attaturk.

President Nasser and Mr. Aly Sabri at the Press Conference held on 12th August 1956

Another scene at the Press Conference. President Nasser and Dr. Mahmoud Fawzy

Dr. Mahmoud Fawzy

Canal in the Liberation Province

CHAPTER FIVE

THE ARAB COMMONWEALTH VISION

I HAD not been in Cairo long before I realized that Nasser and his comrades had a dream so ambitious and far-reaching that it might vitally effect the trend of diplomacy and power politics not only in the Near East but throughout the Islamic world. It is essentially an Arab vision. It is a plan to unite under one flag the Arab world now scattered and dispersed into a number of small, comparatively weak nations, most of whom, like Syria and Pakistan, have only recently received their freedom.

The influence of each member of this vast brotherhood in world affairs must be negligible, but the influence of a united Arab brotherhood would be immense. It would control vast areas, many of them strategically important, it would have great oil wealth, and it would speak, with one voice, in the name of millions of like-minded peoples with similar interests and common aims.

On their ability to see this new force in world affairs as it is, as it may become and in its real authority and potential power, the stability of the Western—and Eastern—world, during the next ten years, may well depend.

In order to secure real Arab unity, all traces of British influence must be removed; all signs of excessive American infiltration, financial or political, resisted; and the French, as the ruling power, must eventually be cleared out of Moslem Africa.

Why has this dream been conceived? Because Colonel Nasser and his friends are realists. They know that, however soon their High Dam may be built, however hard they try to broaden the base of Egyptian agriculture and industry, Egypt's industrial future is not rosy. The United States has huge stocks of cotton undisposed of, cotton itself being fought in world markets by a whole range of new synthetic materials. The best that the Egyptian leaders can hope for is to maintain the economy of their country. At present, the expenditure and revenue, roughly balanced, is 200,000,000

Egyptian pounds. The rate of exchange is a little less than the official 100 piastres to the pound.

The population is dense in the two great cities, Cairo having over two million and Alexandria nearly a million. Trade, especially in the latter city, is largely in foreign hands, though, of course, every kind of control is in Egyptian hands.

That is the situation these men see and they do not like the limitations it imposes. The figures, and the prospect, mean that Egypt, for the next fifty years at least, is doomed to be a small, but strategically important, Mediterranean and African State. How, then, to revive the glories of ancient Egypt? There is only one way—to unite the Arab countries under Egyptian leadership. How strong would the basis of such an alliance be?

It would be very strong. All followers of Mahomet have not only a religion, but a way of life in common. In this respect, they resemble the Jews, Judaism being more a way of life than a religion. They are closely allied in race; and they speak variations of the same tongue: Arabic. So here are the real links, ready-made, that would bind an Arab Commonwealth. They are much closer than the bonds between, say, the United Kingdom, Malaya and Nigeria. They are natural and, it seems to the Egyptian Premier, heaven-sent links that should be exploited for the good of Egypt and the greater glory of Islam. For this crusade has its religious significance as well as its political aims. The cry is "*Allah akbah!*"—the old cry of the conquering Muslim. It is a cry that finds instant and warm answer in the hearts of millions.

How big is the prize at stake? What countries could Colonel Nasser hope to unite, politically, with his own? And would they accept Egyptian leadership? Let me take the first question and see where the vision reaches.

Let us look first at Iraq, one of the smallest of the envisaged good companions. The further we examine Iraq the more neatly she seems to fit into the picture. Historically, as recent investigations at Ur of the Chaldees have shown, the most advanced type of civilization, including the study of astronomy, geometry and extensive land survey, reached a point of perfection in Mesopotamia about 3,000 B.C. This culture spread to Crete, Greece and Egypt. So the first link between Egypt and Iraq is one of great antiquity.

Both countries were part of the old Ottoman Empire and, during this period, had a similar form of government imposed on them by the Sultan. In the early twenties, when the Emir Feisal was crowned King of Iraq, the country was subject to very strong British influence, just as Egypt was when, after the British protectorate terminated in 1922, the Sultan Ahmed Fuad was proclaimed King of Egypt. Since then, Egypt has shaken off British influence more effectively than Iraq, but Iraq feels herself surrounded by more powerful neighbours, and has been less hasty to oust the British until she is strong enough to stand on her own feet. Egypt, protected by the Red Sea, the Canal, and some hundreds of miles of desert to the West, feels more secure.

Iraq's language is Arabic, the second language, English. Although the total population is a little over four million, it is overwhelmingly Muslim. Most of the formerly large Jewish colony have emigrated to Israel. As in Egypt, there is a large Christian minority. Wheat, barley, beans, rice, dates and Indian corn form the basis of an agriculture that is capable of being greatly developed. And, most important factor in power politics, there is oil. The total revenue is some forty million dinars (the Iraq dinar equals one pound sterling), but the expenditure is kept well under the revenue figure. Iraq is solvent and potentially rich; it is Arab and it is Mohammedan. All the requirements are here. So Major Salah Salem, Colonel Nasser's Ambassador at Large, talks to King Feisal of Iraq (and to his Prime Minister) in the friendliest terms, noting how similar Egypt and Iraq are, how common their aims, how identical their ideals.

The same conditions on an even smaller scale are present in Jordan. And here there is a population almost entirely Sunni Moslems, Islam being the State religion.

Nearly half a million displaced Palestinians are taking refuge in Jordan's territory, an immense infiltration when compared with Jordan's own population of under two million. So that Jordan, more than any other country, has helped the displaced Arab refugees whose political cause against Israel Nasser champions.

Jordan's links with Britain were far too close for the liking of the Egyptian Government. Most suspect of all was the British hold over the Jordanian Army, through its officers under General Glubb in the Legion. So King Hussein of Jordan and all his important Ministers received calls from the roving Major Salah Salem, and in this matter, where a change accorded with Jordan's nationalistic feeling, the Egyptians had their way. With a swiftness that portrayed a certain nervousness, Glubb Pasha was removed, with his chief lieutenants. It was a major coup for Egyptian diplomacy, the weird part of the move being that it was, apparently, unsuspected in Whitehall. One wonders what His Excellency the British Ambassador, the first, second and third Embassy secretaries, the Vice-Consul, the Military Attaché, and the Information Attaché were doing at this time. Not, apparently, being supplied with accurate information of the intentions of the Jordan King and Cabinet.

In Saudi Arabia, Colonel Nasser sees a country on the verge of great development and immense oil wealth—largely financed, at present, by American companies, but whose present economy and wealth are at a low level. All the traditional ties are here; the flag of Saudi Arabia has this heartening device in white letters on its green background: "There is no God but God. Mohammed is the Prophet of God." Arabic is the language of ninety-eight per cent of the population, and it is difficult to exaggerate the importance of the linguistic link. It is still true that instinctively we do not take too seriously anything written in a foreign tongue. Arabic is spoken as the primary language in the Sudan, Libya, Morocco, Algeria, Syria and Lebanon, as well as in Egypt, Iraq and Arabia. They speak the same language. It is a first step to realizing the same dreams. The religious ties between Egypt and Arabia could not be closer, for in Arabian territory is Mecca, towards which every Moslem turns as he prays. Before the advent of oil, the Mecca pilgrims, bringing into the country some ten million pounds a year, paid for Arabian imports. There was virtually no foreign commerce. Oil and its development are changing this strange situation almost overnight.

Syria was under a French mandate until she gained her independence during the Second World War. She has adopted an American type constitution (as Nasser is doing in Egypt), her people are Moslems, the language is Arabic. Here the Egyptian leaders feel that the barriers against them are less formidable; British influence is negligible, French influence has disintegrated. Syria is an ally ripe for the choosing.

Apart from Arabia proper, there are a number of small but potentially wealthy minor Sheikdoms where British influence is at present dominant, but where Colonel Nasser has linked his cause to that of local nationalists. These are the Sheikdom of Kuwait, the Kingdom of Yemen, Bahrein, and the Sheikdom of Quatar. All are Arab-speaking Mohammedan States. The Persian Gulf, where the British Government maintains a Political Resident who, through the political agents, acts as mediator and Governor to the Sheikdoms, is split into a number of territories each ruled by its own chief. In every case, the authority of the British political officer is challenged by a pro-Arab pan-Islam movement.

I do not think that the Egyptian vision stops at the Near East. At least it envisages a foothold in the Indian continent, through alliance with Muslim Pakistan. The fact that Pakistan is still a member of the British Commonwealth does not deter Colonel Nasser. These ties, he would say, are artificial. They are the dying bonds of a failing imperialism whereas our ties are real, alive, unalterable. Sooner or later, they must achieve a resulting unity.

How far has Nasser really got in making his dream come true? It is easy to underestimate what he has accomplished. I left Cairo convinced that Egyptian plans are more mature, more detailed, and more practical than the Foreign Office in London would admit either officially or privately.

On March 12th, the Arab League had a long meeting in Cairo. For six days Colonel Nasser sat closeted with the Syrian and Saudi Arabian delegations. Then they issued a statement which, they frankly said, did not contain the whole field covered by the talks, but the salient features: as much, perhaps, as it was thought advisable to make public property.

The British and American press wrote off the statement as adding nothing new to the situation and the known facts, but it seems to me to be of exceptional interest, for it is the first time that the three nations have publicly declared very wide common interests.

It is the community of interests that the document first stresses. Complete agreement was reached on all points, inspired by the "increased consciousness of the Arab nation". I do not know whether the word "nation" is a translation.[1] It is certainly significant.

Referring to the United Nations Charter, all three nations pledge their support of a policy of active neutrality—whatever that may mean. But Arab defence "should spring right from the heart of the Arab nation, in accordance with the requirements of its own security, away from all foreign pacts which try to utilize defence organizations in serving the partisan interests of any of the great powers".

[1] It is a translation. The Arabic word could also be translated as "group".

On the Palestinian issue, the statement can only be described as "cagey". We are told that decisions were taken to safeguard the interests of the Palestinian Arab.

The Bandoeng Conference comes in for specific mention in words that reflect the pride of the Eastern nations in this all-Eastern conference. The principles adopted at the Bandoeng Conference are said to be "a landmark guiding our policy in the international sphere".

The Israeli question is dealt with in these remarkable words: "A comprehensive plan [was adopted for] ensuring Arab security . . . defending it [the Arab nation] against the dangers of Zionist aggression and foreign domination." Defence plans were to be co-ordinated for the three countries concerned against possible Israeli violence and measures taken "with regard to the situation arising out of the attitude which certain States adopted by allowing the recruitment of their subjects into the Israeli armed forces". A decision was also taken over policy towards States supplying arms to Israel.

What the announcement does not reveal is whether there is a firm agreement by the three nations to come to each other's aid in case of aggression. But the general tenor of the talks suggests that there is some such agreement, possibly under a unified Egyptian command.

The Baghdad Pact comes in for severe censure. It is said to be an attempt to divide and weaken the Arab States who pledge themselves to take measures to counteract it. Jordan is not specifically mentioned. Colonel Nasser is not quite sure where he stands with King Hussein and the Jordanian leaders, so the announcement merely says that the conference is willing to assist Jordan to stand on her own and resist pressure to join the Baghdad Pact. It is left to Colonel Nasser's Ambassador in Amman to implement this promise in a more concrete form.

There is a very broad passage that refers to the co-ordination of Egyptian, Syrian and Saudi Arabian interests in the political, military, economic and cultural fields, followed by a contrastingly concrete passage that there is a plan "to face the problem arising from British occupation of the Buraimi oasis and the Oman emirate in such a way as to preserve for these zones their Arab character and to prevent any breach of their sovereignty or of their rights".

French policies in North Africa and her wide dominion there is attacked as abrogating the rights of the Muslim people there, and of being a grave threat to world peace. There is no doubt that Colonel Nasser and his colleagues, free from the irritating restrictions of American, French and British representatives, revelled in the freedom to express their thoughts and ambitions in their own way. The announcement does not tell us all; but it tells us a great deal.

It seems clear that the triumvirate were puzzled by the attitude of the Jordan Government and unsure of how far in King Hussein they had a friend or a foe.

The King's refusal to attend the conference is not mentioned; nor is his proposal for a conference of all Arab States in his own capital. No friendly word is extended to him, only the expression of determination to assist Jordan to stand on her own feet.

Several articles by Egyptian leaders have been published warmly congratulating the Jordan King and Government on the dismissal of General Glubb, who is depicted as an arch-imperialist, a portrait which will amuse the General's friends because of its absurdity.

Since the dismissal of Glubb Pasha, there have been important changes in the higher echelons of the Arab Legion command. It may well be that these changes are not yet complete. A large number of British officers remain at their posts. The Legion is still one of the few efficient fighting forces in the Middle East. Colonel Nassar prefers to wait and watch events, perhaps hastening their course from time to time, if the trend is favourable to him.

In the event of an Israel-Egyptian war, Colonel Nasser would like to count on the support of the Arab Legion. Israel, then, attacked or counter-attacked from the east as well as from the south, would be in dire peril. The five hundred thousand Arabs who have fled from Israel to Jordan would be eager recruits to any patriotic home guard or guerrilla army.

The position in Jordan is too fluid for the Egyptians and their allies to take immediate action. Time, they feel, is on their side.

Colonel Nasser would dearly love to include Persia (Iran) in his plans, but, at present, it seems that Persia has definitely decided to join the Western Powers as a staunch member of the Baghdad Pact. However, it was noticeable that the Foreign Office, during the visit of the Russian leaders to London, talked as if the Baghdad Pact were now "on ice". American influence is strong in Persia; the country has a fascination of its own. But it is not an easy country for either Colonel Nasser or London to anticipate or to control.

Colonel Nasser hopes that he understands the mutations of Persian politics better than we do in Britain, but even he is left puzzled. This is nothing new. The Persian political scene has baffled observers—even those of long residence and experience—from the time when its leaders first played a part in modern Near-Eastern affairs.

At the head of the turmoil and intrigue stands the Shah-in Shah, His Imperial Majesty Mohammed Reza Pehlevi, now thirty-seven, who married, as his first wife, a sister of King Farouk, by whom he has one daughter. He is now married to Queen Soraya, a brilliant and beautiful woman.

Around the Shah are the satellite stars of the Persian political firmament, bright or dim, according to the vagaries of political fortune and the turn of the unpredictable wheel of power.

The country is now, nominally at least, ruled by the Shah as a constitutional monarch, with the help of a Senate, half elected, half appointed, and a Constituent Assembly. But it was obvious, as recently as 1953, when war raged between the outgoing Premier, Dr. Mossadeq, and the incoming Premier, General Zahedi, that the Shah is riding a turbulent tide. All we can say is that, at present, he appears to be able to ride it, being accepted by Persians as the last arbitrator, the referee who has the last word when the battle for power becomes too bloody, or too confused to know, without a decision, who has won.

The present Premier, Hussein Ala, is something new on the Persian scene, for he is admitted on all sides to be a man of complete integrity. This works both ways in Persia. It enables him to be rid of pressures that are ordinarily imposed on the holders of his office. On the other hand, it makes him irritatingly un-get-at-able by the people in Persia who traditionally are used to having the politicians in their pockets.

In these shifting sands Colonel Nasser's men pick their way with care. On the whole their reports are more realistic than those of their Western counterparts. They keep their eyes on control of the Army and the police. Sometimes it seems that the determination of power in Persia can only be resolved by answering the question: "Who can arrest whom?"

As far back as 1952, the Majlis adopted a bill for the nationalization of the Persian oil interests, but in 1956 Persian oil is still, for the most part, in private hands. The Government have published a Seven-Year Plan for industrial development and for a fairer allocation of Persian land and mineral wealth. At the time of writing, its prospects seem fair, but corruption, the traditional strength of vested interest, and the characteristic Persian inclination to postpone all decisions may bog down this plan as they have innumerable others in the last ten years.

Persia's independence is still guaranteed by the Anglo-Soviet Treaty of 1945, which leaves Britain and the U.S.S.R. the paramount Foreign Powers in Persian eyes. This state of affairs is not looked upon as ideal by Colonel Nasser. At the present time, there is nothing that the Arab League can do about it. No one wants to provoke a situation whereby the U.S.S.R., invoking her treaty rights, could re-enter Persian territory (which she occupied jointly with Britain during the war), so it behoves all comers to tread gently in their approach to Persian politics.

Persia's role for the past fifty years has been to play off the East against the West—and she has done very well out of it. Turning her weakness into a bargaining strength, she has been constantly smiled upon by both sides.

Now, at last, she has come down heavily on one side of the fence. Persia has joined the Baghdad Pact. It was a bold step and has been opposed by the Communists, by the Shah's enemies, and by some religious leaders fearful of Christian influence and penetration into their Muslim Empire. But the Shah and his Premier have carried the day. Persia is a friend and ally of the West—unless by some sudden, dramatic coup the situation changes overnight.

Colonel Nasser watches these events with attention and concern. He sees in the Persian relationship with the West, and in her treaty obligations, just that combination of power politics and interference in Arab affairs by the West that he most dislikes. But he does not despair. He waits for the Persian climate to change. For Persia, he would say, has her real links with her Arab neighbours and friends.

The picture I have drawn of Egypt's ambitions in the world of foreign affairs is not the picture that Colonel Nasser himself would put forward when he is talking to foreign correspondents, though I think his testament confirms its truth, and it is not doubted inside

Egypt that this is the path he wishes to pursue, believing it to be his country's right and destiny.

When answering the questions that foreign newspapermen put to him, he pursues, in all sincerity, another line. He constantly states that his policy is neither anti-British nor anti-American. And he believes this. But his belief is founded on the assumption that Britain and America will eventually quit the Middle East, leaving the field open for complete Arab unity. He believes that the Arabs, thus united, will secure the peace of the Middle East, and act as a barrier to Communism much more effectively than the Western allies are able to do by remote control. This point of view is said to have had some impact both in Washington and in London. A good deal of re-thinking is going on, the real question being: could the Arab nations be won as a *bloc* rather than be separately seduced? Or, once united, would they go entirely their own way? And what would be the future of Anglo-American oil interests in these territories? For oil, let us frankly admit it, dominates the thoughts both of the State Department and of Whitehall in this matter. Middle Eastern oil must not be Russian controlled—that is the basic principle in both capitals.

The French, so concerned were they at the turn of events, proposed a conference on Arab affairs to be attended by the Foreign Ministers of the Western Powers in 1956. But neither London nor Washington felt inclined to take this move.

Colonel Nasser, in his interviews with visiting newspapermen, has been quoted as putting his case in this way:

"I am not opposed to British interests. There are many interests which the British and the Arabs have in common, and we should attempt to further them.

"For example, both Arabs and British benefit from the oilfields. We should work for our mutual interests. There is no room for hate between us and without hate Britain will not attempt to destroy my interests and I will not attempt to destroy hers. But I believe that by attempting to keep this area as a sphere of influence, Britain will lose her real interests—do damage to herself. For that matter, we are not opposed to the Northern Tier defence system as long as it is outside the Arab *bloc*.

"After the Baghdad Pact was signed we asked Britain not to spring any more surprises, and when informed that Pakistan was going to join we raised no objections. Nor did we oppose Britain's adherence—we did not regard it as our affair. Britain did not keep her promise when it came to Jordan. She did not tell us of the mission of General Templer (Chief of the Imperial General Staff) and we were forced to fight against all efforts to bring Jordan into the pact.

"If Jordan had joined, Syria would have been cut off, pressure would have been put on her to join and eventually Egypt would have been left alone—alone to face Israel. I did not realize until shortly before I went to Bandoeng last year that Israel was a vital question for the Western Powers. They wanted above everything to protect Israel. The whole Arab world would have been turned to face the north, and Egypt left exposed to the real danger which comes from Israel.

"We had not been thinking very much about the Israeli danger until she became aggressive on our frontier and we learnt she was being armed through France. We wanted our wealth for our own internal developments but were forced to buy arms to meet the threat from Israel. . . .

"I was to be isolated in this area by British policy and was refused arms while Israel armed herself. I was told to look to the United Nations and the Tripartite Declaration, but frankly I have no faith in them. The whole situation could be turned upside down before either of them took any action. In any case, decisions of the United Nations have never been enforced. . . ."

Egypt had no policy, Colonel Nasser said. "All we do is react—react to the activities of Britain.

"This means that the great opportunity for Anglo-Arab relations created by the Anglo-Egyptian agreement in October 1954 has been thrown away. There was a brief honeymoon, and then Britain plunged into the Baghdad Pact plan which she knew in advance was, in our opinion, a threat to our vital interests.

"It was also against the genuine desires of the Arabs. Any policy in this area must recognize nationalism, its historical background and psychological condition. Arabs are not able now to accept themselves as a tail to British policy, and that is how they would regard it if we all sat round the table with Mr. Selwyn Lloyd or Sir Anthony Eden.

"Arabs would be convinced the policy came from London, and this is no longer acceptable to them. It must be realized that the Northern Tier—political front line—will not have any value if the internal front collapses. It is the internal front which will defend the genuine interests not only of the Arabs but of Britain herself. That is why the Arabs must have their own regional organization and base their policy on the strengthening of an Arab collective security pact.

"This view of the internal situation is at the core of my policy, for it seems to me more important than the danger of world war whereon Britain bases her defence requirements. I may be wrong, but I do not expect world war. Nuclear weapons have changed the entire picture, so that any decision to enter war would require extreme conditions beyond our calculation.

"As I see it, war from now on will be different. It will be fought on the internal fronts of all countries. In this area it will use nationalism as a weapon and we—the leaders of this area—must lead the nationalists and build a stable future on them.

"That is what we are doing in Egypt, and as a result we have taken the weapon out of the hands of Communism. Secret Communist pamphlets show this is recognized, for as recently as a fortnight ago, they were attacking me. In universities where Communism was well organized it has no organization at all. There may be a few Communists, but the universities go peacefully about their studies without any security arrangements being necessary.

"Communism is only dangerous when it can exploit the mass opinion of nationalism. There are about five thousand Communists in Egypt, but we have taken the leadership of nationalism away from them. Compare this situation with 1952, when small Communist groups brought about riots and the burning of Cairo. People say there is dictatorship in Egypt, but this is not so. I want to lead the people, not suppress them. British policy—if successful—would make it impossible to lead the people. They would rise up against us all."

Colonel Nassar is astute as well as sincere. He knows that oil is at the bottom of Anglo-American concern in Arabic countries. So he says, again I think without mental reservations of the type we understand, that oil, so far from being a bone of contention, is a common interest. "You want the oil. We want our share of the oil revenues. Let us work this thing together." But the lesson of Abadan is there for all to read. As the Arab strength and unity grew, will they accept this tacit, commercial partnership? Will they not wish to market their own oil,[1] and, as their technical abilities increased, even mine it themselves? If they were able to do so, the Arab countries would be immensely rich, instead of bordering on poverty. So Britain and America are loath to loosen their grip, financial and political, on the Middle East, believing that, in the last resort, the ability to fly in forces to protect their interests is the only sure sanction against their interests being infringed upon. With this type of thinking Colonel Nasser, and, indeed, all the Arabic leaders would most fervently disagree. For this is the old Imperial Power in phantom form hovering over them. One of the most aggravating problems for the Arab States to deal with now is how much technical aid and money to accept and in what form. They are under no illusions. They know that where the old imperialism used guns, the new uses the World Bank and its majority in the United Nations. On such matters Colonel Nasser is a downright realist who tears across the artificial barrage of platitudes about peace and international understanding that act as a smoke screen for power politics. He has set his gaze on Arab unity and words and protestations of peaceful intentions do not, for a moment, delude him.

Finally, Colonel Nasser's vision turns not only to the East, but to the West as well, back into Muslim Africa. "We can never forget," he had said, "that we are part of this vast continent where millions of our faith still suffer foreign domination. The reawakening of Africa will go hand in hand with the resurgence of Egypt."

In Libya, Morocco and Algeria (as well as to some extent in Nigeria, Madagascar and Zanzibar) Arabic is the common tongue, Islam the binding faith. There is no doubt that the Egyptian Government fosters and befriends all movements in these States towards breaking British and French ties. Hence the concern of the French Government, and the anxiety for an immediate conference on Arabic affairs.

The killing in circumstances of peculiar horror of twenty French farmers in the wine-growing district near Oran had horrified French opinion in Paris and in the provinces and has alerted them to the part played by Radio Cairo in encouraging the rebels. While Egyptian propaganda was mainly against Britain, both the Ameri-

[1] It is sometimes said that this would be impossible for lack of transport. We should not be too sure of this. A great many tankers fly the Greek and Panamanian flags.

can and the French authorities assumed a curiously detached attitude. But when it is turned against their own interests, there are the most vigorous protests.

Nasser is quick to see and interpret this kind of reaction. He sees the West as more divided than united in spite of the Baghdad Pact, which he regards as a British conspiracy. He sees that, wherever British influence wanes, the Americans edge a well-heeled shoe through the open door. He speaks to British diplomats and finds their attitude towards Americans "correct", which he thinks is British for "unfriendly". The French supplicate both allies to take action, but both refuse. United? No, Colonel Nasser does not think this is unity. As compared with this open dissension and concealed ill-will, the Arab States, inside the Arab League and outside it, have the warm undercurrent of common aims and a single faith and tongue.[1]

[1] However, apparently a greater degree of unity between America, Britain and France has been achieved at the London Suez Conference.

CHAPTER SIX

THE DAGGER THAT DRIPS BLOOD

THE deep and abiding hatred felt by all the Egyptian leaders for the new State of Israel, at first, shocked and surprised me. I had no particular love for the Jews, but I felt that all nations were entitled to a life of their own, a country of their own, where they could practise their own faith, work and develop their own culture, unmolested. Palestine, obviously, had great historical associations for the Zionist movement. Prior to 1940, some fifty thousand Jews lived there in peace with the Arab majority. I knew that Britain, more than any other State, had been responsible for creating the State of Israel. I was only offended when I heard Jews, who might well be grateful, running down the great powers without whose help and aid no Jewish nation would exist.

On my very first day in Cairo, I asked officials of the Ministry of National Guidance what the Egyptian attitude to the Israeli issue now was. The answer was emphatic. "We are at war with Israel. We always shall be." On returning to the Metropolitan that evening, I made a note of that remark. I believe it contains the naked truth. Egypt may have, expediently, to bow to United Nations pressure and, from time to time, shelve her vendetta, but she will never drop it. Nor will the Arab League tolerate the State of Israel indefinitely. The wrongs done to the Arab world by the new State are too terrible, too numerous, to be either forgotten or forgiven.

Arnold Toynbee, who writes with great constraint, impartiality and judgment, has this to say on the question in his *Study of History*:

"If the heinousness of sin is to be measured by the degree to which the sinner is sinning against the light that God has vouchsafed to him, the Jews had even less excuse in 1948 A.D. for evicting Palestinian Arabs from their homes than Nebuchadnezzar and Titus and Hadrian and the Spanish and Portuguese inquisition had for uprooting, persecuting and exterminating Jews in Palestine and elsewhere at diverse times in the past. In A.D. 1948 the Jews knew, from personal experience, what they were doing: and it was their supreme tragedy that the lesson learnt by them from their encounter with the Nazi German Gentiles should have been not to eschew but to imitate some of the evil deeds that the Nazis had committed against the Jews."

On my return to Britain, and on a recent visit to Canada and America, I found there was a reluctance, almost a fear, to state the real facts concerning the persecution of the Arabs by the Jews in Palestine. An American politician, greatly respected, said: "Yes, we know, but the truth is dynamite. The press here would tear one to bits if one told it."

I am determined not to be put off telling the truth of what I found and, at the same time, to keep detached from the hot, searing wind of prejudice that blows through these Cairo streets.

For instance, not long ago, Jewish batteries, "in retaliation", shelled the market place at Gaza on the afternoon of market day, the only time when it is packed by a close concourse of sweating peasants and members of the public. The Jewish guns succeeded admirably in what they set out to do. Several old women, a number of children, including babies in arms, and a great many men there on business—all civilians—were killed or had limbs blown off. Several little Arab children were blinded.

A few days later Egyptian commandos entered Israeli territory "in retaliation". When I protested that, by doing this, the Egyptians had spoilt their case and sunk to the level of their adversaries, I was told: "If they behave like swine, we must treat them as swine."

In the face of this intense loathing which the Jews have provoked in the Arab countries, in Cairo in particular, Mr. Hammerskold's efforts in postponing the Egyptian-Israeli conflict were an amazing and great achievement which received no adequate recognition in the press, either in Paris, London or New York.

As this question of Arab against Jew is likely to provoke war at any time during the next ten years (I know of no other issue so dangerous unless it is the Far Eastern division of Vietnam), I studied the whole question as deeply and as impartially as I could. It is not possible to understand it, without going back a few years to see how it all started.

I soon realized that the Egyptian attitude was based less on the

Typical Egyptian "fellah"

Suez oil refinery

Village in the Liberation Province

plight of the Arab refugees than on the situation of what has now become the Arab minority (formerly a big majority) in Israel. It is impossible to present a picture of the new Egypt without going to the roots of the Egyptian hatred and this entails understanding exactly what is happening to the Palestinian Arab.

Of the inhabitants of Palestine on the eve of World War I, the large majority were Arabs (Christians and Moslems), while a very small minority of about fifty thousand were of Jewish faith.

Most of these Jews had lived in Palestine for centuries, and had enjoyed there—as in other Arab lands—as secure and unmolested a life as their co-religionists had enjoyed in the most tolerant of Western countries.

The remaining Jews had come into the country since the latter part of the nineteenth century, largely to escape persecution in Europe. They had clustered together in settlements of their own, yet the reception which the Arabs had accorded them had been hearty. Indeed, even after the so-called Second Aliyah (i.e. second immigration wave) of the first years of the twentieth century, which had been promoted by the newly-initiated Zionist movement with the objective of establishing a "national home" in Palestine, the Jewish settlers continued to receive a hospitable welcome. The situation began to change only when the Zionists decided to dispense with and boycott Arab labour, as the revealing reminiscences of Mr. Ben-Gurion, recently republished in his *Rebirth and Destiny of Israel,* candidly admit.

From that point on, especially after the announcement of the Balfour Declaration, the Arabs came to see in the expanding ranks of Jewish settlers a threat to their own national existence. Declarations like Dr. Weizmann's statement in 1919—that the purpose of Zionism was that "Palestine would ultimately become as Jewish as England is English"—served only to underline the threat and to convince even those Arabs, who had preferred to give Zionism the benefit of the doubt, of the basic incompatibility between Arab national aspirations and the objectives of the Zionist movement.

The history of the succeeding decades—1920 to 1948—is a story of persistent Arab struggle for survival and dignity.

To come now to the present situation. The United Nations envisaged Arab and Jewish States in which the rights of Jews and Arabs respectively would be guaranteed and observed. Specific provisions to this effect had been included in the Partition Resolution.

In direct violation of the elementary principles of human rights, and of the specific provisions of the Partition Resolution, the 175,000-odd Arabs of the Holy Land who had stayed behind after the expulsion of the greater majority of their fellow-countrymen have been subjected to patent discrimination, in law as well as in practice. This discrimination is in sharp contrast to the oft-repeated assurances of Zionist leaders prior to the establishment of Israel, as well as to the relevant statements in Israel's Proclamation of Independence.

The oppressive and discriminatory policy which the Israeli government has systematically adopted towards the Arabs under its control manifests itself in civil, personal and political rights: economic and cultural rights; religious rights; and property rights, as the following paragraphs show. But perhaps as important as the official governmental discrimination is the popular and unofficial persecution of the Arabs in Israeli-held territories. Thus Mr. Hal Lehrman speaks of the need for the Israeli government "to protect them [the Arabs] against the hostility of certain Jewish elements, particularly those veterans who return to a housing shortage after military service against the Arabs, and those immigrants who exchange a European DP camp for an Israeli transit camp." And Mr. John Cogley makes a clear distinction between the protective provisions of the law and the "undercurrent of ill-feeling"—which is "not a matter of law" but rather a "question of atmosphere". Mr. Cogley also emphasizes the failure of the Israeli authorities to curb terrorists and extremists, whose hostility to the Arabs often expresses itself in outrageous acts. He says:

"No one in authority in Israel has proposed that these murderous private citizens be tracked down and punished. As is true in the earlier case of the frightful Deir Yassin massacre, and in the killing of the U.N. mediator, Count Bernadotte,[1] terrorists have gone scot-free again; worst of all, apparently no one in authority is even vaguely interested in apprehending them."

Concerning the official policy and actions of the government, the following facts, based on the testimony of fact-finding visitors, may be established.

Civil, personal and political rights: The nationality law of 1952 regulates the granting of Israeli citizenship. It openly applies two

[1] The Jewish clique who organized the murder of this great and good man have not until now been named or charged.

yardsticks: one to Jews, and the other to Arabs. Citizenship is automatically granted to Jews, upon whom the unrestricted "right" of entry into Israel is conferred by the Law of Return of 1950. On the other hand, Arabs can receive citizenship by virtue of residence, naturalization or birth, and in each of these methods special conditions have to be fulfilled.

Thus, in order to obtain nationality, an Arab must have been included in the official register before January 1952, (although whole Arab villages had been by-passed when the authorities carried out the registration of the inhabitants); must prove continuous residence in Israeli-held territory since the establishment of the State; must have a knowledge of Hebrew and, finally, must be approved by the Ministry of the Interior as worthy of Israeli citizenship. It has been estimated that no more than ten per cent of the Arabs of Israel would quality for citizenship under this law, on which William Zukerman commented in his *Jewish Newsletter*:

"Whether the figure is ten per cent or twenty-five per cent, the nationality law, in principle, is sharply discrminating against one section of the population as compared with the other. Jews, the majority of whom are immigrants of a few years' residence in Israel, may become citizens automatically. They may even hold dual citizenship. . . . But the 170,000 Arabs in Israel, who have lived on that soil for centuries and have never left it, are limited in their rights to acquire citizenship. A more flagrant case of discrimination is hard to find even in the annals of the chauvinistic twentieth century."

Even those Arabs who do obtain Israeli citizenship, however, are distinguished officially as "Class B citizens". "They have to carry a special Class B identification card," writes Mr. Cogley, "which clearly marks them off as non-Jewish Israeli citizens at all times."[1]

Referring to this discrimination, Dr. Harold E. Fay wrote in the *Christian Century*:

"Israeli citizens carry an identity card bearing a number. On the cards carried by Arabs, the number is followed by the letter B.[1] That small letter sometimes makes a big difference."

Furthermore, the areas in which Arabs are concentrated have been placed under military rule in which the Ministry of Defence exercises authority. Galilee, the Negev, and the so-called Little Triangle,

[1] How slavishly the Israeli Government have followed the Nazi pattern is shown by this lettering device.

with a population of 145,000 Arabs (out of a total Arab population of 175,000) are thus under direct military rule.

"The residents of these governorates live within a matrix of legal restrictions which fix their movements into, out of, and within the area, and give the army authority to banish legal residents and to confiscate their property, remove whole villages from one zone to another, and to try in military summary courts individuals who violate its regulations," writes Don Peretz.

"All Arab communities are under military government and only Arab communities are," observes Rabbi Morris S. Lazaron.

"Every area in which Arabs are in a majority is under military rule. . . . The harshness of the military constitutes a major source of complaint by the Arabs," reports Dr. Fey.

The consequences of placing the Arabs under military rule are manifold. Civil rights are virtually suspended. The Israeli government dismisses "due process of law" when proceeding against the Arabs: "Individuals are banished from their villages, permanently or temporarily. Others are imprisoned by military edict for not co-operating with police investigations, on suspicion of harbouring infiltrators, or even if they are just believed to be 'troublemakers'," observes Marian Pearl.

The military government sentences suspected infiltrators and believed troublemakers "without trial, on the basis of the emergency regulations" reports the *New York Times*. "The Arabs have no *habeas corpus*," states Rabbi Lazaron. Even against the criticism of the press and of the Supreme Court, the government of Israel maintains its policy of "collective punishment" of whole Arab communities for acts committed by individuals.[1]

One consequence of military rule is the restriction of movement, applied strictly against the Arabs. For example, "the Nazareth resident who wants to visit a relative in Jaffa must apply for a military permit to leave town a day or two before his trip. This involves filling in application forms, a trip to the Military Governor's office, and waiting in line for hours, all of which may eventually result in failure," reports Mr. Peretz. "Not even the Arab members of the Knesset have freedom of movement," states Rabbi Lazaron. "An Arab cannot even go from Nazareth to Cana, a distance of six miles, without a permit," writes Dr. Fey.

Even within the same city, restrictions of movement apply. Mr.

[1] Himmler's favourite form of retaliation against the Jews.

Hal Lehrman describes the situation of the Arabs of Jaffa—formerly a city of over 75,000 Arabs, but now inhabited by a majority of Jews with less than 5,000 Arabs as follows:

"The Arabs are concentrated inside the small but neat Ajemi quarter; they live in kind of reverse segregation; they need passes to go out, and Jews need passes to go in." He writes in another context: "It may be a peculiar word to use but 'Ghetto' is the one I think of for the guarded enclosure where Arabs are concentrated in Jaffa and other once-important towns."

Not only are the Arabs discriminated against in their enjoyment of their elementary civil and personal rights, but they are also denied basic political rights. "They have no real political parties of their own," writes Rabbi Lazaron; "they are not adequately represented in the government, and the road is closed to their securing such representation," reports Dr. Fey. "Only four of their local councils have been elected by village residents, while the others—where they exist at all—had been appointed by the government," reports Mr. Peretz.

Finally, it must be mentioned that Arab affairs are handled by more than a dozen governmental ministries and departments—a situation which has obvious unsalutary consequences. It has often been said by Israeli spokesmen that, notwithstanding all these considerations, the Arabs of Israel can always resort to the courts of the land in order to secure justice. Entirely apart from the high cost of, and the long time consumed by, resorting to the courts, and also apart from the obvious fact that the courts must decide in terms of the existing laws of the state, it must also be mentioned that often the decisions of the courts go unheeded by the authorities, particularly the military. As Rabbi Lazaron puts it: "The military forces at times ignore even the decisions of the highest Israeli courts. For instance, an Arab takes his claim to home or land to court. The court confirms his claim and orders his property restored. The military destroys the property on grounds of 'security' and no one does anything about it."

Dr. Fey, citing a number of concrete instances in support of his statement, says that "court rulings in favour of Arabs are frequently by-passed or circumvented," and that, while "the high court of justice often rules in favour of the Arabs," at other times, "it will simply refer their complaints to the high military tribunal, where they die."

Economic, social and cultural rights: The "job opportunities" of Israel's Arabs are "rigidly restricted", according to Mr. Cogley, and there are differences in wage scale between Jewish and Arab Israelis." "There are two price levels for agricultural products, one for Israelis and another for Arabs," asserts Rabbi Lazaron.

Patent discrimination is also exercised in the educational facilities available differentially to the Arab and Jewish communities.

Dr. Fey comments as follows on the educational facilities provided for the Arabs: "Although they pay taxes and subscribe to the compulsory loans on the same basis as other citizens, their schools are the poorest in the country. Text books are scarce and the teachers are unqualified. Many teachers are Iraqi Jews, who speak Arabic, but are not well trained."

Religious rights: Speaking for the Evangelical Episcopal Community in Israel, the Reverend Rafiq A. Farah wrote: "Some of the property of this community is still in the hands of the Custodian of Absentees' Property."

On February 26th, 1953, Monsignor George Hakim, Archbishop of the Greek Catholic community in Israel, told the Hebrew daily, *Maarev*, that "many church properties are still illegally seized, priests are not allowed permanent residence in Israel, and religious students are prevented from reaching theological schools." Mr. Cogley states that "Catholic nuns and priests . . . . complain of being viciously insulted—even spit at—on the streets and mocked even by quite small children."

As for the Muslim community, its Waqfs (i.e. religious-philanthropic communal properties) are controlled by a Jewish appointee of the Israeli government. According to Rabbi Lazaron: "The State has taken over the property of the Waqfs, the Muslim institutions of charity. Surely the administration and control of such properties should be in Muslim hands. The liaison between the Muslim communities and the State is in the hands of a government official who is not a Moslem but an Israeli Jew. Surely the Moslems should have the basic right to appoint one of their own faith as liaison officer in dealing with the government and the right also to administer such affairs as their charity and philanthropy."

Last, but not least, the confiscation of Arab property by the Israeli authorities must be cited. A number of laws successively enacted by the Knesset authorize the government to confiscate the property of the refugees, the property of those Arabs who, while still living inside Israeli-held territory, are residing in other than what were, on May 15, 1948, their normal places of residence, and even the property of Arabs who had not moved from their homes.

According to Mr. Peretz, "about four million dunams (880,000 acres) of Arab-owned land were taken over by the Israeli Custodian of Absentee Property. Of this area, approximately 300,000 dunams belonged to Arab residents of Israel who had fled from one section of the State to another during the fighting, or had been moved from their villages by the Jewish authorities for 'security reasons'."

In addition to all these manifestations of the discriminatory policy of the government of Israel, mention must be made of the destruction of inhabited Arab villages, by the armed forces of the State, for the establishment of settlements for incoming Jews, or in retaliation for acts allegedly committed by some members of the village concerned. The interested reader will find in the pages of *Ner*, (a monthly periodical published by the Ihud Association in Israeli-held Jerusalem) for example, detailed descriptions of countless instances of such retaliatory destruction or expropriation of the farmland of Arab villages.

To achieve this cherished end, the Israeli authorities have resorted to the application of measures hitherto unheard of in modern times.

First, in order to clear the tables and pave the way for ultimate confiscation, the Military Governor declares, as a first step, an Arab area a prohibited zone. Having done so, another step is taken to ensure that no Arab is allowed to enter the prohibited zone and proceed with the cultivation of his land. This done, the 1953 law is evoked and agricultural lands become liable for confiscation since the owners have failed to tend and till their lands themselves. But, since the owners are barred from reaching and cultivating their lands which have already been declared a prohibited zone, the confiscation becomes an accomplished fact. This means that the property of the Arabs automatically becomes the property of the State. And when land becomes the property of the State, a nominal compensation is offered to the owners. Since the rate of compensation per acre is less in value than the income of a year's yielding of the land, the Arab owners decline to accept the offer. The total areas confiscated in this way exceed 1,100,000 donim.

A similar process is applied to the land and property of those Arabs known to the world to-day as "refugees" and who are not allowed to return to their homes and lands. The Israeli authorities had appointed a special sequestrator to administer the lands and property of the refugees, ironically classified as "absentees". The special sequestrator pays income tax to the Israeli treasury. He is also the sole arbitrator who fixes the rate of the income tax.

Having appropriated the land, and property of the "Arab absentee", the sequestrator takes the next step and contacts the "Development Council" with a view to offering for sale the land and property of the "Arab absentees" for a nominal price. When the transaction is made, and the property transferred to the Development Council, the Council in turn invites Israelis, business concerns and companies to buy the property, usually for exorbitant prices. The profit thus gained goes into the Israeli coffers.

It is quite clear that Israel had adopted this most unusual process in dealing with the property of the Arabs in order to give this absurd proceeding the semblance of legality. They hope by so doing, when peace comes, the Arab refugess will have been compensated for the loss of land and property on the basis of the price rate fixed by the sequestrator when making his deal with the Development Council.

This is Israel at work. What a vast contrast between this and the claim made in some quarters that Israel represents the most democratic, equitable and progressive area in the Middle East!

Writing shortly before the establishment of Israel, Dr. Weizman said: "I am certain that the world will judge the Jewish State by what it will do with the Arabs."

In the light of the evidence marshalled in the preceding pages, one may perhaps be permitted to wonder when Dr. Weizman's prophecy will be fulfilled.

Colonel Nasser feels nothing more strongly than he does the essential unity of the Arab peoples. The abominable treatment meted out to the Palestinian Arabs within the State of Israel infuriates him. It seems grotesque that the Jews, so recently released from race persecution and the whole vile machinery of the Gestapo by British, American and Russian Armies should, almost within a decade, be practising the very same odious doctrines themselves. There is not a single malpractice of the Jewish government to-day that had not its counterpart and inspiration in Nazi Germany.

In addition to the fate of the Arabs within Israel, there is the life led by the Arab refugees. There are nearly a million of these, according to the last censorship taken in January 1956. There seems no immediate prospect of the number being decreased. The plight of the Arab refugees should shake the conscience of the world. As I visited these huge, drab camps, I was reminded, most vividly, of my four years spent in a Japanese prison camp. These people were not in fear of death, but they were without anything that could be called a life. The hopelessness and despair of feeling unwanted, useless, a burden, of being fed like beasts who cannot be allowed to die: that I saw, and I felt I could have cried out to the complacency in Whitehall and in the State Department which allows this great sub-nation to continue to exist in this terrible way. Nor are Britain and America only to blame.

Whatever Colonel Nasser's reactions, he is powerless to do more than mitigate the situation. But the United Nations, by a united imaginative effort, could end this living horror. One of the imminent causes of war would then be removed.

No experience of mine in Egypt had anything like the impact on me that arose from the searing hatred of the Egyptians for the State of Israel. I felt that, when I wrote of it, it was of small account that my report might be criticized as one-sided or biased; what was important was that I should get the truth, as I saw it, on paper.

Whatever I now read in the newspapers, whatever the United Nations reports say, I know that Egypt and her allies will, some day, go to war with Israel. Their object is to blot out the State of Israel which, to them, seems a monstrous creation. Yet the Egyptians and the Jews have much in common, and while I write these words, the large Jewish population of Egypt, collected mainly in the great cities, is living in peace and personal friendship with its Egyptian neighbours, free to pursue their own way of life, including their faith, their work and the enrichment of themselves if they can.

When I realized this, I knew that it was Jewish barbarity towards the Arab, not prejudice against the Jews as such, that was stirring this shot-blast of hatred. It would, some day, bring a fearful retaliation against the small, new State of Israel which, if wiser counsels had prevailed, could be an example to the world, of courage, of faith and of the innate genius of its people.

CHAPTER SEVEN

LAND FOR THE LANDLESS

NASSER and his closest comrades of the Revolutionary Committee belong, almost without exception, to the fellaheen class. They are Egyptians, usually with little admixture of Turkish or Sudanese blood, and they are close to the people, close, in particular, to the peasant, the working peasant, the very small farmer.

As soon as they had banished Farouk and suppressed all overt opposition in Cairo and in Alexandria, they turned to the land, from which they or their immediate forbears had sprung, and planned one of the greatest schemes of Socialistic land reform that this century has seen either in the East or in the West. Their declared objects were to correct the lopsided Egyptian economy, to abolish the aspects of land tenure loosely described as feudalism, and (though this subject is not mentioned), to build up, for future years, popular support for the Revolution in the hearts and minds of the fellaheen: a support so broad and so strong that it might perpetuate the Revolution indefinitely.

In order to carry out this daring and fundamental project, Nasser ordered the latest figures on land ownership to be brought up to date. These were the figures presented to him and they showed, quite clearly, how great was the task to be tackled.

Size of holding	Number of landowners	Total area held 1,000's feddans
Under 1 feddan[1]	1,981,339	770
Over 1 to 5 feddans	617,860	1,324
Over 5 to 200 feddans	159,347	2,661
Over 200 to 800 feddans	1,835	625
Over 800 to 1,000 feddans	92	87
Over 1,000 to 2,000 feddans	127	220
Over 2,000 feddans	61	277
	2,760,661	5,964

[1] One feddan is equal to one and one-third acres.

The last ruler of Egypt to go to the root of the land problem and to create a virtual Domesday Book was the first Mahommed Aly. Between 1813 and 1818, he issued edicts which had two main objectives.

The first was to prevent any peasant disposing of his land. As soon as the crop was gathered in, he had to deliver it to the State granaries. It was weighed and measured, and its price fixed, by the Government. The second objective was to ensure the payment of tax in cash or in kind. But no money was paid to the peasant. He was provided with seeds and fertilizers but no money. This made him a financial slave. The balance due to him was paid in the shape of State bonds. In theory these could be redeemed, but in practice, neither Mahommed Aly nor his successors honoured their bonds. The fellah was bound hand and foot. He could live: that is, he could be born, breathe, work, marry, bear children and die. From the earth he came: to the earth he returned, and never once in his life had he the feeling of independence and free choice that money can give.

In the next hundred and forty years the grip of the dynasty on all the land of Egypt loosened, yet King Farouk and his family still privately owned nearly twenty per cent of the total cultivatable land at the time of the Revolution. This gave Nasser his cue. The easiest land to requisition belonged, of course, to the Crown, but requisition was by no means confined to previous royal property.

The Land Reform Law was promulgated on September 9th, 1952. It was the first measure of reform taken immediately after the breakdown of the old régime on July 23rd, 1952. The first article in the law provides that no person can own more than 200 feddans.

Any contract involving contravention of this provision is considered invalid and cannot be registered or enforced.

The chief aim of this law is the abolition of agricultural feudalism and the redistribution of arable land on equal and equitable terms by limiting ownership to 200 feddans. The law gives the owner the right to transfer the ownership of 50 feddans of his land to each of his sons, provided the total so disposed of to his children does not exceed 100 feddans.

The land requisitioned by the enactment of the law is not taken over from its holders without indemnity. The indemnity is equivalent to ten times the letting value of the land: in the form of

Government bonds, bearing interest at three per cent, redeemable in thirty years.

The new landowner pays the price of the land in annual instalments within thirty years with the addition of: first, the value of buildings; secondly, an annual interest of three per cent; thirdly, fifteen per cent additional expenses.

According to the law, the letting value of arable land in Egypt is assessed at seven times the basic tax. About seventy-five per cent of farmers have taken advantage of this article. Article 32 of the law provides that "the land may be let only to those who work in agriculture".

Article 33 provides that "the rent of the land may not exceed seven times the basic tax. And, in case of share-cropping, the share of the owner must not exceed half without including expenses."

The total survey of land subject to Land Reform Law and including the confiscated land of the ex-royal family (according to legislation No. 598 issued in 1953) amounts to 621,479 feddans, whereas the whole arable land in Egypt is about 5,974,784 feddans.

Nasser's Land Reform, which at present has a five-year schedule, is fascinating as well as fundamental. Before the new law was promulgated, a detailed inventory of land, buildings, stock, crops, and machinery was made, and it is clear that the emancipated fellaheen are to be very strictly supervised by the Government.

The opposition in Egypt are already saying that he has merely substituted one master for another. That, whereas before he was the slave of his feudal overlord, now he is, in effect, the servant of the Government.

On the whole, I do not think this criticism justified. It is almost impossible to prevent abuses and bribery where power in the country villages and outlying districts is exercised by petty officials, but the intention of the leaders of the Revolution is to liberate their compatriots, not to introduce them to a new bondage.

The fellaheen, for centuries, has been accustomed to autocratic rule. He understands an order, not a request. To some extent, the Government have had to recognize this and to use it in putting through their reforms.

How paternal and even stern the hand of the Egyptian Government still is in dealing with its peasants is shown most clearly in its organization of the Liberation Province. Like so many schemes in Egypt, from the earliest times, the Liberation Province has been conceived in the grand manner. Its conception goes back to the days immediately after the Revolution.

On April 5th, 1953, the Revolutionary Government decided to create the Liberation Province in the area to the left of the Delta, flanked in the north by the Nubaria Canal and in the south by the Desert Road. The area of the province is now 610,000 feddans, which will increase to 2,200,000 feddans in the future.

The project was examined and prepared for execution by the best specialists in Egypt. They studied the project on a purely scientific basis and came up with the greatest plan the East has known in modern times.

The main canal for the province was dug and the hills flattened; work proceeded towards reclaiming the desert with two aims in view:

The first was to increase the area of arable land in Egypt from five per cent to ten per cent, by rehabilitating the cultivated areas; by lessening the pressure on areas which are heavily populated; and by providing a means of living for thousands of people who will settle in the province. The second aim was to improve social standards by creating a new generation proud of their motherland; and by laying the foundation of a new rural society which will eventually provide the rest of the country with experts to carry out the new agricultural policy throughout the country.

The area where the new Liberation Province is now situated was chosen for five reasons. It is close to the other cultivated areas lying on the western bank of the Nile; it lies midway between Cairo and Alexandria, the two main cities of Egypt; communications with other places in the Republic are available; its sandy earth is good for cultivation, and artesian water and building materials are also available in this area.

The Liberation Province will consist of small holdings: five feddans to the ordinary farmer and ten feddans to a university or agricultural college graduate. The inhabitants will wear a uniform dress. Each village has 230 houses—the house is made up of two rooms, a bathroom, a kitchen, hall and backyard. Everybody will receive adequate education. Particular care will be given to the clothing and social welfare of the inhabitants.

The province will be irrigated from a big canal which receives its water from Rayah El-Beheiri.

The authorities have given the problem of water supply great attention—water-pipes, canals, artesian wells and artificial rain[1] are all being used to make an arid area a fertile province.

Experts, architects and social workers will use every sort of agricultural and building machinery: tractors, pumps, power stations, factories, smithies and every other convenience are being made available so that the province may stand on its own feet. In many ways the province is a self-sufficient area.

After the completion of the first stage, 35,000 feddans will be ready for cultivation. The second stage, ending in 1958, will add another 166,500 feddans to the cultivated area.

The third stage will begin after the High Dam project has been completed, and will add another 400,000 feddans to the province.

In other words, the Liberation Province will have a cultivatable area of 600,000 feddans. There will be 428 villages each having 1,400 feddans, 1,150 of which are for cultivation. The rest will be used for buildings and parks.

What sort of society exactly is envisaged in the Liberation Province? Is there to be any liberty apart from the province's name? At first sight, to Western eyes, there seems to be an extraordinary degree of regimentation. The workers will wear the same uniform, live in identical houses, farm identical strips of land, work similar hours, plant similar crops, be supervised by the same Government experts and even enjoy recreation in the same communal centres.

There does not seem to be much room for rugged individualists in the Liberation Province. It will be neat, tidy, productive, efficient; but will it be free?

The answer is, I think, that so vast a project—and it is vast in conception and execution—could never be carried out, with the human material available, unless the most comprehensive planning was made and executed by a central authority. The conditions under which the Liberation Province farmers will live may seem to us over-regulated and confined, but they represent a great advance on anything they have been used to before. If and when the new constitution is really operative and the political parties' bill promulgated, the Liberation Province farmers will have political freedom.

[1] Egyptian experiments in artificial rain-making are said to be in advance of other countries.

In the meantime, they will have security, a modicum of comfort; and they will have begun to live.

The intense organization of the province will make it very easy for the Government to control and guide the political thoughts and ambitions of its increasing population.[1] The whole area could, quite easily, be cut off from all contact with outside influence and news. The dangers are obvious, but so, too, are the opportunities of success. So here, again, we must give credit for a daring, bold conception, and trust that the years will bring liberalism to the central Government which, in turn, would hand it on to the people of the Liberation Province.

In Britain and America, we are always applying the "freedom" test to all new ventures. It suits us to do so, for we have developed economies and social structures that enable liberty and great reforms to go forward hand in hand. Egypt has not yet reached that stage of development. The only way Nasser can hope to bring these mammoth plans to fruition is to impose them from above, hoping that the people will capture the vision as he sees it and back it by their brains and work. To some extent, this has happened, already. The whole Land Reform project of the Government, the Liberation Province in particular, has fired popular imagination.

When the fellah receives his ownership deed, giving him new lands and new responsibilities, he takes it home proudly, frames it and hangs it high up near the ceiling in a place of honour, where it displaces the portrait of King Farouk. It is placed side by side with the portrait of Nasser; and the man and the deed, together, represent in the mind of the peasant his benefactor and his gift.

There is no doubt that, apart from the sly, silent political factions in Cairo that dare not raise their heads at present, the main opposition to Nasser will come from the large landowners whose estates are threatened by the new laws.[2] The compensation scale, from their point of view, is hopelessly inadequate. They protest in the first place that they have no desire to sell to the Government or anyone else. The cultivatable area of Egypt—the Nile valley—is very small, but it is rich, and those who are lucky enough to hold large areas of it are desperately anxious to keep their holdings. So this

[1] It is fair to say that the Liberation Province, in its inception and its execution, is a social, not a political, venture.

[2] The Suez Canal issue has, more recently, united all classes.

law strikes at their most precious heritage. Nor have the large landowners any great faith in Government bonds. They say that these depend for their realizability and worth on Colonel Nasser's régime, whereas the land endures for ever. Finally, they say that their money is tied up for decades and that the interest rate of three per cent is ridiculously low. It certainly is, as compared with the rates of interest obtainable in Egypt for private "crop loans".

I found that it was common practice for the fellaheen, at certain periods of the year, to borrow at five per cent per month for, say, four months and that the loan documents were ferocious. Not only was the total interest due over the whole period deducted from the loan before it was paid, but the lender, in the event of default, became the owner of the total security, in some instances worth three or four times the value of the loan.

Finally, in Cairo, in circles unfriendly to Nasser, it is being said that the administrative difficulties of the land reform project, as at present envisaged, are so great that the whole scheme will collapse in confusion. I do not believe that this is so. There is a great deal of wishful gloomy thinking in this matter. Colonel Nasser and his colleagues, having raised the hopes of the fellaheen so high, dare not now disappoint them. And, apart from this, the leaders are genuinely determined to drive their reform, in which they sincerely believe, through to success.

To achieve this it has been necessary to do much more than merely create the Liberation Provinces, and organize wholesale redistribution of big estates.

By putting new life into "Crédit Agricole d'Egypte", the Government has largely overcome the curse of usury in Egyptian agriculture. This institution was founded twenty-five years ago.

A royal decree was issued on July 25th, 1931, creating the Crédit Agricole d'Egypte with a paid-up capital of £E.1,000,000 represented by 250,000 shares of £E.4 each, half of which was subscribed by the Government. The latter guaranteed a dividend of five per cent to the other shareholders and undertook to make loans to the new institution up to £E.6,000,000 at a low rate of interest.

According to its statutes, the Crédit Agricole carries out the following operations for the benefit of agriculture, either to agricultural co-operative societies or to individual cultivators: (1) short-term loans for the expenses of cultivation and harvesting of crops;

Village and allotments in the Liberation Province

Bulldozers at work in the Liberation Province

Sand levelling in the Liberation Province

President Nasser being greeted by the people on his return from the Bandong Conference

(2) distribution of fertilizers and seeds on credit to all cultivators. It is worth mentioning that seeds and fertilizers before their distribution are examined by the technical departments of the Ministry of Agriculture to make sure that they fulfil the necessary conditions as to the power of germination and the degree of cleanliness of seeds, as well as the required percentage of the fertilizing ingredients of manures. (3) Loans to agricultural co-operative societies and small cultivators against agricultural products. The primary object of these loans is to stabilize prices of products by enabling cultivators not to market the crop immediately after harvest. Loans are generally fixed at eighty per cent of the current price and no cover is due in case of a fall. (4) Medium-term loans for periods not exceeding ten years, comprising loans for the purchase of agricultural machinery and cattle; and loans for the reclamation of land. Loans for agricultural machinery and cattle are granted to co-operative societies against the personal guarantee of their boards of directors, while loans for the amelioration of land are granted to small landowners against a mortgage of the land.

During the war and up to the present time, the Government, with a view to controlling the distribution of cereals, has entrusted the bank with operations which do not come within its normal field of work, such as buying for the Government's account the quantities of requisitioned cereals: wheat, rice, barley, maize, etc., which cultivators are bound to deliver according to quotas fixed on the basis of the fertility of their land.

These products were transferred from rural districts to the centres of consumption. The bank also took over the delivery of foreign wheat and maize imported from abroad to cover the deficit of local crops. Thanks to the many stores (Shoonas) belonging to the bank, scattered all over the country, very big quantities have been handled.

According to its statutes, the Crédit Agricole was charged with rendering services to agricultural co-operative societies. As there are other kinds of co-operative societies which are in need of credit facilities and of an institution to carry out for them all kinds of banking operations, it was thought necessary, in 1949, to entrust this task to it, introducing the necessary additions and modifications into its statutes in order to enable the bank to become the general credit institution for agriculture and co-operation. Its name was, therefore, changed to "Crédit Agricole et Coopératif" and its capital was increased by £E.500,000, half of which was subscribed by co-operative societies and the other half by the Government.

In order to render its services to agriculture and co-operation with ease and promptness, twenty-three bank branches were created in the capitals of provinces and eighty-three sub-agencies in the rural districts. Furthermore, in order to facilitate the distribution of seeds and fertilizers, and depositing agricultural products, the bank possesses 550 fertilizer stores all over the country.

The bank has become an important factor in the economic life of the country, serving both agriculture and co-operative movements.

The services of the bank to the land reform scheme is of paramount importance because, as a result of the break-up of vast estates, co-operative societies have become essential for its success.

In every branch of the society's activities, the advances for fertilizers, as well as for seeds, and general purposes, the value of the society's loans has risen rapidly both to co-operative societies and directly to individuals. With regard to the latter, some amusing stories are told. The point of the stories is that if you know the right people in Egypt and elsewhere, facilities are open to you that are closed or completely unknown to the general public.

The Nasser Government has been very anxious to encourage alternative crops to the cotton crop. Even with their High Dam project eventually realized, they know that cotton alone can hardly keep Egypt solvent, far less prosperous. So they are pressing hard in other directions.

The propagation and distribution of selected rice seed is a favourite project of Colonel Nasser. This project is to be executed over a period of three years, starting with the 1953 crop. The first stage has already been carried out. The use of these seeds is expected to result in an increase of about twenty per cent over the present yield. This, besides answering the needs of local consumption, will provide a surplus of high-quality rice, fit for export. The Council has set a committee to study the expansion of rice cultivation by using water from artesian wells. Remembering how easy it is to lose a rice market by improper mixing of the grades of rice (as was done by the Chinese in Thailand and Malaya) the Government have further schemes for labelling and marketing crops.

Another favourite project is sugar beet, which can be grown profitably in areas which will grow little else. The Government entrusted an Egyptian stock company with the execution of this project. It will reclaim 30,000 feddans in the Nubaria district which will be devoted to growing sugar beets and establishing a sugar factory and a refinery capable of producing 60,000 tons of sugar a year.

The capital of the company is £E.5,000,000 and members of the staff and workmen of the refinery will be entitled to a fixed proportion of the profits and the company will build suitable houses for them. The Government has undertaken to provide the necessary irrigation water for this project.

To round off their agricultural policy and help along its basic reform of land distribution, the Government has had to pay particular attention to pest control and measures against animal diseases. Both were abnormally high in Egypt, incurring losses that, to us, seem fantastic.

Because of pests and insects, Egypt suffers an annual loss of £E.37,000,000 in crops. The Permanent Council for the Development of National Production has recommended that the necessary funds be provided for combating pests and insects. A sum of £E.880,000 has already been earmarked for this purpose in the 1955-56 budget.

Under the old régime, Egypt failed to provide the proper means for storing cereals. As a result there was a loss of £E.4,000,000. To prevent this, the Government has decided to build two big silos, one at Alexandria with a capacity of 30,000 tons, and another at Cairo with a capacity of 40,000 tons. The cost of both is estimated at about £E.250,000. The Government has allotted £E.100,000 as a preliminary sum to the company undertaking the construction.

The country has been divided into zones, each of which will be provided with a veterinary unit undertaking the care of 20,000 animals. The first stage of this scheme, which includes the construction of thirty new units is, in fact, an extension of the present eleven units. The cost of this stage is £E.189,000. £E.13,500 more are allotted to veterinary laboratories.

With the majority of Egyptians engaged, either directly or indirectly, in agriculture, and with cotton, rice, sugar and maize as the life-blood of the Egyptian economy, Colonel Nasser, by breaking up the large estates, has gone to the root of the unbalanced Egyptian social and economic system.

The word fellah means a ploughman or cultivator. The Moslem fellah is pure Egyptian and he is a stable political factor. This cannot be said either of the nomadic Bedouin of the south or of the Nubian of the Nile valley, who are of mixed Arab and Negro blood and are most populous in the district between Aswan and Wadi-Halfa. The fellah, who has been placed in the racial category of Hamito-Semite by the scientists—is hardworking, uncomplaining and conservative. If he has a latent sense of humour, during my visits to Egypt I never unearthed it, but it is said that after harvest he relaxes for a time and sets aside a few days for love and—if he is not too strict in his faith—drink. If he is a morose and humble man now, it is only because the dead weight of the centuries have made him so. He has never been a slave, but serfs of medieval England were merry freemen as compared with him.

Premier Gamal Abdel Nasser has taken the fellah to his heart: the cause of the fellah is now bound up with the fate of the Revolution. To make this clear Nasser has travelled the country districts, where he was received with every sign of love and gratitude by the fellaheen. In Khartoum and in Tewfikia he made speeches on his great reform and they were the most sincere speeches that this man has made in Egypt. I quote from his Tewfikia speech:

"The principal object of our Land Reform is to liberate our country from the octopus of feudalism which, throughout the ages, has symbolized political bondage.

"Since the days of Mahommed Aly, the political life in Egypt has been based on full and rigorous control of the fellaheen—the majority of the Egyptian people. Now freedom is yours.

"This great reform has not been conceived overnight, but is the outcome and fruit of the silent struggle of years. The revolutionary leaders—all of the fellaheen class—are determined to shatter the whole system of feudalism and semi-slavery.

"It is you, the fellaheen, who constitute the real revolution, not me with ten or twelve colleagues. The forces of reaction have already surrendered. This reform is going through to the end. Treasure, then, your new possessions; cultivate them with your toil and your skill; protect them with your lives."

Both speeches were received with frantic applause by huge crowds.

The banners bearing the inscription: "This is Your Land" were borne away in triumph by the crowd, and Colonel Nasser, who seemed touched and happy at his immense ovation, turned to a colleague and said: "We are winning. It is to be a real revolution of the people, not merely a *coup d'état*."

CHAPTER EIGHT

COTTON, OIL AND THE NEW INDUSTRIES

I HAD the opportunity of talking, both in general terms and in detail, to a large number of business men in Egypt of all nationalities. Most of them acknowledged that the new Government had set to work energetically to improve the Egyptian economy, but, they said the Government's plan involved spending vast sums the Government had not got, and they added that the restrictions on imports and the tiresome rules governing the issue of import permits made the smooth running of an Import/Export business very difficult. I, myself, checked on the last complaint and I found that it took anything from a day to three weeks to obtain an import permit.

The truth is, of course, that Colonel Nasser's Government would like to see Egyptian trade in Egyptian hands. They realize that at present this is impossible, but their ambition does not make them treat the local foreign merchant with any special consideration. Only when the business brings in direct hard currency to Egypt, as in the tourist business, is the way made smooth and the atmosphere friendly. I must say that the more I knew of Egyptian business the more I sympathized with the Government's view. It is a constant aggravation to see foreigners in sole control of efficient, profitable business concerns. The fact that they work hard, have invested their own capital, is easily lost sight of. What strikes the average Egyptian is the thought: "I could do that. Why have I no chance to do so?"

Both the Cabinet and the Ministry of Commerce were very much concerned with the two basic matters of oil and cotton. On her cotton exports Egypt's prosperity depends. Up to now she has produced little oil, but her ambition to become a first-class power, and her natural jealousy of the oil richness of other Arab States has stimulated the Egyptian leaders into a drive for oil that may revolutionize her oil position.

Egypt under her new régime has recently instituted a new forward-looking policy for the exploitation of the nation's oil resources, thus ending the period of uncertainty in the oil industry in Egypt which has persisted for over five years. Egypt is not as rich in oil as some of her Arab neighbours, but she is keen to exploit her deposits to the full.

The new agreement concluded between the Government and the four largest oil companies operating in Egypt has opened a new era. The agreement means fresh development and exploration plans, modernization of existing refineries and installations which will involve the expenditure of millions and will mean much new capital investment. That the oil interests have every confidence in Egypt has been shown by their willingness to invest large sums over the coming years.

The agreement was signed after some eighteen months of the most intricate negotiation and was hailed in Egypt as the turning point of her domestic oil industry. Owing to the absence of other fuels in the country, Egypt has great dependence upon oil for her industry, her agriculture and her domestic life. Importation of oil has meant a heavy drain on her finances.

There is also a complete range of petroleum derivatives which have become increasingly important in recent years, both for the manufacture of chemical products and in combating plant diseases. These derivatives have already made significant contributions to the advance of agriculture, and scientists are convinced that further research in oil and its products can bring further benefits, especially in the fight against the insect menace. Further, increased mechanization of agriculture, which is now being strongly encouraged, will make heavier demands upon the supply position of the commodity.

Plans are proceeding for the extraction of electric power from the Aswan Dam, but present estimates show that, when this scheme is complete and working, it can only meet some twenty-five per cent of the national need for power and so oil must remain the prime source of power in the foreseeable future. At the same time as its claim for oil, the whole mineral wealth of the country is being assayed. This includes iron, phosphates, manganese, chrome, asbestos and gold. There is an efficient Government oil agency at Say.

The agreement reached with the foreign oil companies shows that, at present, Colonel Nasser has to rely on them to find his oil and to work it. Egypt, of course, is only one field in the world network of prospecting that British and American Oil Companies undertake.

The test will come if and when good quality oil in quantity is found in Egypt. The present Egyptian Government will expect a share of the oil profits as well as royalty percentages. However, the Companies are strong, if they hold together which, for the sake of their shareholders, they have to do in a project of this kind.

At the Ministry of Commerce I was given the official résumé of the Egyptian policy on Petroleum apart from the Government's agreement with the Oil Companies. In order to convey the optimism that pervades it, I reproduce it as it was handed to me.

"Petroleum is the second most important primary material upon which industry in Egypt depends. There is no coal in Egypt and power has not been developed in the past. But even after generating hydro-electric power from the High Dam, petroleum will remain to be one of the chief elements necessary for the development of industry in Egypt.

"Petroleum products constitute 87% of the fuel used in industry—in U.S.A. it only constitutes 66% while in England petroleum products form only 14% of the fuel necessary for industry.

"Our oilfields meet only 68% of the demand of local consumption. The rest is supplied from foreign sources and costs us 12 to 13 million pounds of foreign currency yearly. This fact will be aggravated by time if we consider the inevitable expansion in the fields of mechanized cultivation, industry and communications. Our consumption of oil products at present increases at an annual rate of 10%. It was therefore incumbent on the Government to lay down a comprehensive policy for the production, refining and storage of oil.

"In the first place all laws concerning petroleum prospection were revised. Law No. 66 of 1953 was therefore issued regulating the new conditions for oil prospecting in Egypt. This encouraged oil prospecting firms to come to Egypt in search of new oilfields.

"Before, all prospection was centred around Suez Bay and the shores of the Red Sea. Now oil prospection activities extended to the Western Desert.

"With the help of the Permanent Council for National Production the Government examined all the stages through which the petroleum industry goes. They encouraged the establishment of an Egyptian Company for the transport of petroleum products, the first of its kind in Egypt.

"There are two oil refineries in Suez; one belongs to the Anglo-Egyptian Oilfields Refinery; the other is a Government refinery which was extended to produce 1,300,000 tons annually. Its output was limited to 300,000 tons before extension.

"Another refinery was established in Alexandria and will begin working next year.

"The Permanent Council for the Development of National Production has allotted the necessary funds for the establishment of a bottled gas factory (Butagaz).

"Oil derivatives are transported to Cairo from Suez by railway as well as by specially-equipped trucks and river barges. These means of transport are quite expensive. The Government has therefore decided to lay a pipe-line from Suez to Cairo. Work on this project has made much progress and it is expected to be completed by the end of next year.

"This will be in addition to the 6-inch pipe-line which the Egyptian Government took over from the British Forces, in accordance with the Anglo-Egyptian Agreement on the Suez Canal Base.

"The new policy also provides new stores for oil where it is mostly used. New stores are being built and the oil ones are expanded. Two sites in Cairo and Alexandria have been chosen for the new stores. The Egyptian petroleum policy is now aiming at a market objective."

At present Egypt has to pay hard cash for her oil and it is one of the highest figures on her import list. But the desire to become an oil-producing nation goes far deeper than anxiety to avoid paying out currency, or even to benefit from oil revenues. It is linked up, inextricably, with Colonel Nasser's ambitions for Egypt. If he is to dominate the Arab world and lead the Arab nations, Egypt should in every way equal or surpass her allies. She does so now in nearly every field. The only card that the smaller allies, such as Iraq and Saudi Arabia, have that Egypt has not, is oil.

That is why Colonel Nasser eagerly reads the reports on the possibilities of oil in the Western Desert. So far oil survey has been confined to the Suez and Red Sea areas, but, quite recently, some remarkable reports came in from a small group of prospectors in the Western Desert. They were kept secret. The report was considered so promising that large scale operations in the Western Desert were authorized. There seems every likelihood that, within the next two years, the American and British Oil market will react favourably to very important oil discoveries in Egypt. The work is being pressed on with extraordinary energy and determination.

Oil, as I write these words, is still a dream for the Egyptian Government, even if it is a dream soon to come true. In the meantime Egypt has to live, and she lives by cotton. Here there is real difficulty, and the future is not bright. The United States is holding huge surplus stocks of cotton. Substitutes are gaining steadily in favour in the world markets.

The most remarkable feature of the Egyptian cotton export recently has been the fantastic jump in exports to Czechoslovakia, Hungary and Switzerland. The "Iron Curtain" countries now take over a third of the Egyptian cotton crop.

There is no doubt about the significance of this. Egypt, baulked of her cotton market in the West, is turning to the Russian satellite countries to absorb her surplus. And they, on terms favourable to themselves, are glad to take immense quantities. The jump in export to Czechoslovakia is prodigious. From 1st September, 1954 to 5th January, 1955, it was 13,560 bales. During a similar period this year it had jumped to 30,000 bales. In other words, Egypt now depends on the "Iron Curtain" countries for maintaining her economy to a vital extent. Whether it would have been desirable, by Anglo-American Government action, to have avoided this, I do not know, but exactly the same trend has developed in cotton that took place when Britain and the United States failed to supply Egypt with arms and ammunition.

I have seen the official correspondence in this matter, and I can understand how vexed the Egyptians became. The outburst that greeted the supply of arms to Egypt by the Soviet Union and her Allies was hypocritical. We had the chance to supply; we did not do so.

One of the first aims of the Revolution was to create a new industrial Egypt. Its purpose was to make the average labourer aware of what industrialization can do for him and how it serves to raise his standard of living.

Industry has now affected every aspect of life, including agriculture itself. The agricultural criterion upon which the Liberation Province had been created is closely connected with the industrial idea of complete self-sufficiency. This criterion also aims at creating industries based on agriculture such as dairy products, sweets, jams, etc.

Some of the most important industrial projects conceived and executed by the Revolution are:

(1) The ammonium nitrate fertilizer factory. This plant will absorb the greatest part of the electric energy generated from the Aswan Dam. It will have an annual output of 370,000 tons of fertilizer containing azote, which may be extended to 500,000 tons to meet the ever-increasing demands of the farmers. It will cost around 24 million pounds. The offers of the various companies which desire to take over the project are now being studied.

This project will save about £E.12,000,000 in foreign currency which were normally used in importing fertilizers.

(2) The raising of the annual output of the calcium nitrate fertilizer plant at Suez to 25,000 tons by supplying it with gas which will be available after the expansion of the oil refinery at Suez, if this gas is needed.

(3) The contribution towards increasing the output of the superphosphate factories at Abu Zaabal and Kafr Zayat to the maximum.

(4) The Jute industry. The project aims at producing 20,000 tons of jute sacks annually. The programme is to be executed in five years starting from 1955. The present factory owned by the Egyptian Jute Company will specialize in hessian products (5,000 tons per year), after it has been furnished with new looms.

A new factory will be constructed to produce 15,000 tons per year This project will cost about £E.2,000,000 contributed by the Industrial Bank, the Pakistani Organization for Industrial Development and the company which will provide the machinery. The present company will contribute all its present assets.

(5) The Paper Industry. The Council has asked various international and local companies to submit their offers for the establishment of a paper and printing industry dependent on the agricultural residue. These are the main points planned by the Council for the development of this industry.

The Revolution leaders did not stop at all this, but have also established factories which have actually started production in the following industries: Railway trucks industry; car spare parts industry; tyre industry; water pipes industry; electric cables industry; nails industry; batteries industry; medicines and pharmaceutical industry.

Colonel Nasser has a concrete, but imaginative mind. He is that rare combination of visionary and man of action and, when he surveys the Egyptian industrial scene, he sees that dependence on cotton is a weakness. Besides, the "imperialists" were always insisting that Egypt was, and should remain, an agricultural State. This, and self-interest, impels him to attempt the industrialization of Egypt.

The Egyptian leaders see that the industrial wealth of the United States is being built on iron and steel just as that of Britain was. They are also exceedingly well-informed of the immense effort made by the Soviet Union to strengthen her economy in this direction hand-in-hand with her development of a New World in Siberia. If Egypt is to become great she must have the sinews of greatness, and here again the Government is driving its schemes with great resolution.

Foreign experts have always tended to assert that Egypt is an agricultural country, without any chance of being even partially industrialized. To this day, sixty per cent of the population are engaged in agriculture.

It was one of the most important objectives of the Revolution to industrialize the country and open a new way of life based on industry.

The most important is the iron industry. In 1953 the Permanent Council for the Development of National Production decided to build a steel and iron factory with an annual output of 220,000 tons.

The Government signed a contract with the German Demag Company for this purpose—an Egyptian stock company was formed with the following as shareholders: The Government; the Permanent Council for the Development of National Production; The Misr Bank; the Industrial Bank; Misr Insurance Company; The Misr Spinning and Weaving Company and The Demag Company.

The factory was constructed on a site south of Helwan—the plans have been already drawn up by the Demag Company.

Work has begun and in three years' time the factory will have reached its maximum output. The raw material will be brought from the district east of Aswan.

The Bahria oases are also rich in iron ore. Since coal is necessary for the reduction process, an agreement has been reached between the company and world firms to supply the necessary coal for a period of ten years.

In its first years, the factory will produce 235,000 tons of iron and steel casting, the value of which, according to import prices, is estimated at 9,000,000 pounds.

Secondary products will amount to some three-quarters of a million pounds.

Coal will cost one-and-a-quarter million pounds—with another million pounds for machinery and raw materials. This means that by producing her own iron and steel Egypt is saving seven and a half million pounds annually.

This will also mean that other industries depending on steel and iron will not be threatened any longer by shortages often experienced in the world markets. Minor industries depending on steel will have more and cheaper steel.

These new industries will provide a means of livelihood for more than 4,000 skilled labourers.

Factories for agricultural machinery and industrial purposes will also be established in Egypt.

Between 1946-1952 machines were imported costing £E.260,000,000.

An Egyptian stock company has been formed to establish the industries, which have already started production of water pipes, electric cables and nails.

The local production of these articles will save the country a good deal of foreign currency.

The Permanent Council for the Development of National Production has secured for these factories an adequate supply of rolled steel and pig iron. These companies were once threatened by a deficiency in scrap iron on the local market. The Council has also decided to establish a railway wagon factory in Egypt, as well as another for the production of motor car spare parts. These projects will be carried out in the very near future.

What must the verdict be on Egyptian industrial and commercial activity? I have no doubt that we must say: Here is a people who are determined to develop their economy to suit themselves. Let us see how we can fit into that picture. We failed to fit into it when we refused to supply arms to Egypt. That would only have been excusable if our object had been achieved—to limit armaments in the

Middle East and restrain both Egypt and Israel. But we must have known that if we procrastinated long enough—and the negotiations dragged on for months—the Soviet Union would make offers. From the Egyptian point of view, our refusal to supply them with arms was not attributable to any desire to mitigate the possibility of war with Israel, but to determination to keep modern weapons in the Middle East in our own hands.

In spite of all the difficulties, the East still presents business opportunities for clever young men from Britain and the States. I have two friends; both left London with less than one hundred pounds; one is now the proprietor of a successful Cairo business, the other owns a motor spare-part manufacturing firm in Bombay. They both left England less than five years ago, they both now have personal fortunes of over ten thousand pounds. These things still do happen. It is not necessary for young people to confine themselves to regions where their own flag flies. Egypt's industrial growth, now vigorously stimulated, offers great opportunities to foreigners who are willing to play the game according to the rules. Those rules are sobriety, honesty, intelligence and loyalty to the government of the country in which they are working, and from which they expect to gain wealth.

In spite of an element of premature optimism in Egyptian official statements on their industrial projects, in spite of the fact that bribery still exists (on a greatly reduced scale) in Egyptian commerce, and in spite of the natural limitations of the Egyptian economy. I returned from Egypt deeply impressed by the business-like determination of the Government to put their house in order, and achieve industrial success on a scale and in directions hitherto thought impossible.

CHAPTER NINE

THE CANAL

It was the seventeenth of November, 1875. The Prime Minister, seated at the chair of his desk, in his room in the House of Commons, was writing to the Queen, who was, as usual, at Windsor. A messenger stood nearby, for the letter was urgent as well as important: "The Khedive appears desirous of parting with his shares in the Suez Canal," Benjamin Disraeli wrote. "He says he must have 4,000,000 pounds sterling by the 30th of the month. Scarcely time to breathe! But the thing must be done."

The Prime Minister continued his letter, in that intimate, conversational style which he found enabled the Queen to grasp the essentials of high policy, and which the Queen found entrancing, so unlike the dreary memoranda of her alternative Prime Minister, Mr. Gladstone, with his plebeian reverence for facts and details. The Queen noted in her diary: "Mr. Disraeli tells me *everything*."

In fact, the Prime Minister, who had the sagacity of the ages, but who yet could be described, accurately enough, by André Maurois as "that eternal spirit of spring", for his heart was young and his vision bright, had not thought it expedient to tell the Queen the whole story. The difficulty was the House of Commons. The Tory hierarchy, which included many of the greatest English landowners, had accepted Disraeli as their leader because his light shone so brightly that it dimmed those of his stolid rivals for the Premiership of Britain, at that time the most influential political office in the world; but this did not mean that the Tory Party as a whole was enamoured of all his ideas. Many were thought to be nebulous and impracticable. The Suez Canal, in particular, had aroused the scepticism of the rank and file of the Party, who saw good British money disappearing into the supple hands of the wily Khedive. One member had referred to the Canal as "that stagnant ditch". The back-benchers, with their craving for a cliché they could understand, snapped up the phrase, and it stuck.

On reflection, Disraeli knew that he could not get the money from Parliament within the month. He himself had said, "The duty of an Opposition is to oppose", and his opponents had taken his advice. Apart from Whig opposition, he would have to contend with opposition within his own Party, with what was, in fact, the earliest "Suez group". He decided there and then to borrow the money privately, to present Parliament with a *fait accompli*, and to repay the lender, as he could, before the expiration of his term of office. Dispatching the letter to the Queen, he sent another messenger to the City, with a note to Mr. Rothschild, asking the financier to come and see him. He came the same evening and Disraeli, placing his cards on the table, showed him the Khedive's request, adding: "I need the £4,000,000 straight away." Rothschild said merely: "I will see what can be done, sir." The following day he was back and told the Prime Minister, not without a touch of pride, "We have the money available." The two Jews shook hands. They had changed the course of history. For Britain was to become the owner of 353,504 out of the 800,000 shares of the Suez Canal Company. It is not a controlling interest, but it was the largest single interest, and carried with it the right to appoint nine British Directors out of thirty-two, the balance being sixteen French, five Egyptian, one American and one Dutch.

The Canal had been completed just seven years when Disraeli made his deal with the Khedive. De Lesseps had finished his work in 1868. It had taken great imagination and determination to achieve this.

The 106 miles of the Maritime Canal, linking Port Said in the Mediterranean with Suez in the Red Sea, is some 200 feet across at its narrowest and up to 500 feet at each of its thirteen turns. Ocean-going vessels, with a draught of up to thirty-five feet, can use it. The passage of the vessels causes constant erosion, although they are piloted very slowly by a highly skilled, and highly paid, corps of international pilots. The dredging and maintenance of the Canal accounts for a substantial portion of the revenue derived from tolls on the shipping using the passage. But the advantages to the world's ship owners are incalculable. Disraeli had realized that the opening of the East, both Far and Near, to Western traffic and trade, was going to result in an ever-increasing stream of seaborne cargoes, bringing the wealth of the East to the West, and bearing the machinery and manufactured products of the West to

Ships passing through the Suez Canal

Another view of the Canal as seen from the bridge of a ship

The Asswan Dam

the East. The journey from London or Bristol to Bombay would be cut by more than 3,000 miles, by avoiding the long and dangerous journey round the Cape. In New York and Boston, American business men, for the first time taking an active interest in world affairs, noted with satisfaction that the Suez Canal would reduce the return journey from Boston to Karachi by 7,000 miles. It was obvious that the whole level of world prices in the West, as well as in the East, depended on the free use and maintenance of the Suez Canal.

This was why the Great Powers of the day, Great Britain, Germany, Austria-Hungary, Spain, the Netherlands, Russia and Turkey, signed a convention at Constantinople on October 29th, 1888, the first article of which reads: "The Suez Maritime Canal shall always be free and open, in time of war as in time of peace, to every vessel of commerce or of war, without distinction of flag.

"Consequently, the high contracting parties agree not in any way to interfere with the free use of the Canal, in time of war as in time of peace.

"The Canal shall never be subjected to the exercise of the right of blockade."

Article Nine of the convention charges the Egyptian Government with the duty of taking the necessary measures for ensuring the execution of the treaty; while Article Thirteen reads:

"With the exception of the obligations expressly provided by the clauses of the present treaty, the sovereign rights of His Imperial Majesty the Sultan and the rights and immunities of His Highness the Khedive resulting from the Firmans, are in no way affected."

It will, of course, be realized that, at this time, the Khedive, as ruler of Egypt, was subject to considerable control from the Sultan at Constantinople, who was the head of the Ottoman Empire of which Egypt formed a part. That is why the Firmans (the edicts of the Sultan) on certain matters were operative in Egypt.

From October 29th, 1888, the date of the convention, to October 19th, 1954, when an agreement was signed at Cairo between the Government of Great Britain and the Egyptian Government regarding the Suez Canal base, a great many agreements had been arrived at, each agreement being followed by its tail of appendices and letters between the Foreign Ministers of the countries concerned. During the whole of that period, the Suez Canal Company operated and maintained the Canal with extreme efficiency, managed by its board of thirty-two directors of five nationalities. Apart from the large British Government interest, most of the shareholders were, and are, French. The head office of the Company was situated in Paris, its executive offices in Egypt. The Suez Canal Company is an Egyptian company, by which is meant that it is registered in Egypt, according to Egyptian law. Both banks of the Canal pass, throughout its entire length, through Egyptian territory. The right to nationalize the Suez Canal Company, which might be thought to be a right inherent in Egyptian sovereignty, which all the treaties declared specifically protected, was not excluded in any of the treaties, though it well might have been. In other words, Egypt never undertook not to nationalize the Company, but by her agreements with Britain, so recently signed, she did undertake to allow a considerable body of British technicians to maintain the former British base which Britain could re-occupy under Article Four of the Treaty of 1954 "in the event of an armed attack by an outside Power".

The principle of Egyptian ownership of the Company as well as of the Canal does not seem to have been disputed, for it was envisaged that, on the expiration of the present agreement, in 1968, Egypt was to take over complete control.

What was it that had occurred in world affairs that caused Western Governments to react so strongly when, on July 28th 1956, Colonel Nasser issued his law, nationalizing the Company? The first paragraph of Article One of the Nationalization Act reads: "The Compagnie Universelle du Canal Maritime de Suez (Egyptian Limited Company) is nationalized. Its assets and liabilities are transferred to the State and the Boards and committees at present in charge of its administration are dissolved."

Article One goes on to state: "The shareholders and holders of founders' shares will be compensated for their shares on the basis of their value at the closing price on the Paris Stock Exchange on the day preceding the date of the operation of this law. The payment of this compensation will take place after complete delivery to the State of all properties of the nationalized company."

The assets of the Company outside outside Egypt are very large and the British Government immediately froze the assets of the Company in London.

On July 29th, the Egyptian Embassy in London issued a statement from which it is clear that Colonel Nasser's decision to exercise his right to nationalize the Company instead of waiting for the period stipulated by treaty was prompted by the American refusal to supply financial aid for the Aswan High Dam project. For nearly a year, major contributions towards the total cost of building the dam (approximately £400,000,000) had been offered by the World Bank, the American Government and, for a token amount, by the British Government. The 18th June, 1956, marked the departure of the last British troops from the Suez Canal area, according to the 1954 Anglo-Egyptian agreement. The Egyptian Ambassador in Washington was instructed to inform the United States Government that Egypt was accepting Western aid to finance the Aswan High Dam. The response was totally unexpected. The Egyptian envoy was told that the aid was no longer available. The reason given was that "at present" the Egyptian economy did not appear to justify the loan. But it is fair to comment that the Egyptian economy had not changed in any material particular between the time when the aid was offered and the time when it was abruptly withdrawn. What appears to have happened is that the American and British Governments had reversed their decision to back Colonel Nasser's régime in Egypt. It was a decision that is having pregnant and far-reaching results.

Colonel Nasser was faced with a situation that appeared to him to be intolerable. The Aswan Dam project, described by Mr. Black of the World Bank, as the "greatest work conceived by man", forms the basis of Colonel Nasser's plan to deal with the root evil of Egyptian economy, namely, a rapidly multiplying population and a contracting market for Egyptian cotton. Already, against her wish, Egypt has had to barter approximately one-third of her cotton crop to Czechoslovakia and other Eastern European nations in return for the military equipment and machines she needs. She would have preferred to sell this cotton for dollars or for sterling in New York or in Liverpool, but the demand was not there. Colonel Nasser decided that Egypt would have to build the dam herself or face increasing impoverishment and an even lower level of living in the years ahead. The Canal was a glittering prize. The hundred-odd miles of tepid water provided a path for the world's shipping in ever-increasing numbers and ever-increasing tonnage. Approximately one-third of the ships using the Canal fly British flags. The other large users are Norway, Denmark, Germany, the United States, France and Holland. The tolls show an ever-increasing revenue. This amounted in 1955 to approximately £35,000,000 or $100,000,000. The Canal is the most profitable stretch of water in the world, carrying nearly three times the commerce of the Panama Canal. American economists have calculated that, with the whole of this revenue diverted to the Egyptian Government, by exercising the greatest restraint in other directions, Colonel Nasser might be able to do three things. He might, with a reasonable amount of aid from the Soviet Government or other sources, be able to complete his High Dam project, while having sufficient money available to compensate the shareholders of the Company and to maintain the Canal efficiently. It does not appear that Egypt would have the resources to improve the Canal by big capital expenditure in order to meet the tendency towards greater draught in modern tankers.

The whole question of the Suez Canal and its control has taken on new significance and importance, because of the vast development of Near-Eastern oil. There is nothing that perturbs the powers-that-be in Washington and in London more than any move that might be constructed as a threat to the free and economic transport of their oil. Western economy, as well as military power, largely depend on this. How vital the Suez Canal is in deciding the price of oil and other commodities may be seen from the fact that a ship paying £4,000 in Canal dues saves approximately £20,000 and fifteen days of time by avoiding the voyage round the Cape.

The Prime Minister, Sir Anthony Eden, in a broadcast[1] to the British people and the world on the Suez Canal situation, suggested that Colonel Nasser's action constituted a threat to the basis of the convention of 1888 and of all subsequent treaties by imperilling the free and open use of the Canal. He noted that Colonel Nasser had ignored United Nations' requests that ships of the State of Israel should be allowed to pass through the Canal. The Government of Egypt does not recognize the State of Israel. Colonel Nasser's reply to the British Prime Minister might be summed up in the words: "We would be the last people to stop ships passing freely through the Suez Canal, because from these very ships we shall derive the money to build the Aswan Dam, which you and America have now refused us."

[1] The Prime Minister's personal attack on President Nasser did more than anything else to augment Arab unity on the Canal issue. It was not until Mr. Menzies made his grave, but dignified television speech that the full seriousness of the situation was realized in Cairo.

The British case rests on the assertion that Colonel Nasser, by character and temperament, is too volatile a person to be entrusted with the sole control of an undertaking so vital to so many people in so many lands. The reaction of the French Government, concerned not only for their ships but for their numerous shareholders, is to back the British Government completely. The reaction of the Soviet Government is to say that their sympathies must lie with Egypt, attempting to get rid of what may be regarded as the last vestiges of Great Power domination over Egyptian affairs. The American Government has taken up a stand somewhere between the two. President Eisenhower and Mr. Dulles have both said that they hope that the future of the Canal will be settled by negotiation, not by force. The Indian Prime Minister has protested against the use of force, or forceful preparations, in Britain and France. The Arab League nations have, on the whole, supported Colonel Nasser, declaring that nationalization is the inalienable right of sovereign States. In this declaration, both Washington and London see a direct challenge to their Near-Eastern oil interests developing. For if Colonel Nasser can nationalize the Suez Canal, why could not, for instance, Iraq nationalize British and American oil and pipelines? Already Iraq, unexpectedly, had given support to Colonel Nasser's cause. This, perhaps, is the most surprising development in the whole affair, for Iraq has been regarded as a key-member of the British-dominated Baghdad Pact and a loyal supporter of Britain in the Near East.

The question of Suez has been complicated by the vast British base including air-fields and supply and operational bases, originally covering an area nearly fifty miles square and having centres at such key points on the Canal as Suez, Ismalia and Fayid. By the treaty of 1954, most elaborate arrangements were made for the maintenance of these bases after the withdrawal of British troops, and it might be thought that Colonel Nasser's action constituted a threat to the bases rather than to the free navigation of the Canal.

Another factor that deeply perturbs the Western Powers is the possibility that Colonel Nasser, if the Egyptian Government were short of funds, might be tempted to increase the tolls on ships using the waterway, without prior consultation.

This is the complex situation that has arisen as a result of the long history of the Canal with its attendant agreements, culminating in Colonel Nasser's act of nationalization. However this situation is resolved, it seems clear that a chapter has been added, strengthening the resurgent movement of the Arab States, which is the underlying theme of this book. I have described this movement, leading in the future to a form of Arab federation, as the most exciting and important international event since the fall of the Japanese Empire. I think that more is involved in this matter than even the important issues of Canal control, which are dividing Britain and Egypt.

It seems that, in the near future, the Western Powers may have to adjust their assessment of world affairs by admitting to their calculations a new power, Arabic, Islamic, and comprising the hundred million people who live between Egypt and Pakistan. If this is so, then the greatest restraint and understanding would seem to be desirable, for the new force, in its inception, might well be more dynamic, and perhaps more chauvinistic, than either the Communist movement in Russia or the slowly developing political democracies of America and Britain.

All foreign correspondents in Cairo are unanimous in saying that, on this matter at any rate, Colonel Nasser has the warm and loyal support of all classes of the Egyptian people, so that to say, as the British Prime Minister did in his broadcast, that the quarrel was with Colonel Nasser alone, not with the Egyptian people, seems to be as near to talking nonsense as a Prime Minister should allow himself to approach. It is obvious that the sequence of events, as outlined in this chapter, is now being obscured by a certain amount of prejudice and passion on both sides, in a large number of countries. One can only hope that wisdom will prevail, so that, without a war, which might have disastrous repercussions, de Lesseps' canal will be kept "free and open, in time of war as in time of peace, to all vessels without distinction of flag".

CHAPTER TEN

THE HIGH DAM

EGYPT has become accustomed, in her long history, to gigantic projects which dwarf the works of Europe and America. The Great Pyramid covers fifteen acres, is nearly twice the height of Westminster Cathedral, and involved the carrying and setting, with the most minute precision, of over two million vast blocks, each weighing between two and three tons. No man since has even conceived such a project, far less been able to carry it out. The Pharaohs who built in this way, and on this scale, could only do so because they owned, in a literal sense, the land of Egypt, and the bodies and souls of their people. They reigned as gods and, as wrathful gods, they ruled. Great working parties, often chained, would accomplish in a day what, under normal circumstances, would have taken them a week. The alternative was death. The lives of the workers engaged on the project was from three to five years. Those who contracted diseases were thrown out to die. If a complaint was made that to carry out a certain order was impossible with the number of slaves available, half would be slaughtered. The surviving half took the hint, and completed the work within the given time.

Apart from such drastic punishments, the slaves were, from morning till night, lashed as they worked. Under such treatment their spirits were soon broken and they became animals indistinguishable from other beasts of burden. The Great Pyramid might be said to have been made by animals for a god.

The Egyptian Information Department in A.D. 1956 is fond of saying that the High Dam to be built some five miles south of the present Aswan Dam—built by British engineers in 1902 and, until now, the chief irrigating agent in Egypt—will revolutionize the life of Egypt, creating a great new industrial area in the barren lands of Northern Egypt where, however, coal is available. What is certain is that the project, if pursued, will certainly absorb Egyptian energies, and manpower, for fifteen years to come.

But will the dam be built? Two obstacles have to be overcome first. There is every indication that both will be surmounted, but, at present, they are formidable. The first is: Where is the money to come from? The second is: Will a firm agreement be reached with the Sudan on the division of the waters available? There is a third difficulty which, I was told, the Egyptian Government do not regard as serious. The vast inland sea created by the Dam will flood the town of Wadi Halfa, which was a small village when Kitchener made it his headquarters in his operations against the Mahdi, but is now a township of some twelve thousand people and, moreover, innumerable unique and ancient monuments will be covered by water. But the real difficulties are finance and agreement with the Sudan.

Mr. Eugene Black, of the World Bank, has described the High Dam simply as the biggest thing ever created by man. At present "created" is the wrong word. The Dam itself is not yet under construction, but exploratory boring and extensive survey have been made according to plans already drawn up in detail.

The first thing that the visitor to the Dam site notices are two barges. From these, the engineers and other technicians conduct their boring operations of the river bed. The rock formation has been found at a far greater depth than was expected. For over a hundred feet at this point the river bed is sand, and this has led to an amendment of plans, for the Dam will have to stand on sand; and the exact composition and qualities of the sand are all-important.

There is a houseboat moored close by which provides none too comfortable quarters for the men working on the project and on the bank; close by is a neat, white office building proudly signposted "HIGH DAM PROJECT".

The proposed area of the Dam can be seen from white lines painted on the river banks. The Dam is to average 250 feet in height and three miles in length. Moreover, the white marks show where a large number of tunnels will come out from the banks.

It is estimated that fifteen power units, each over 100,000 horsepower in capacity, will be in constant operation. The tunnels on one bank are meant to convey water down-stream, those on the other bank to drive the huge turbines. The chosen position of the High Dam is one of the driest and least fertile sites in the Nile valley. There is no village or township in the district and a notable lack of vegetation. Man has deserted this barren area until now.

Or at least he has done so for thousands of years, for up-stream the temples of Philae can be seen obtruding from the water, not yet washed away by the seeping pressure of the inexorable river.

All this is now to be changed. The Dam reservoir will flood the whole of the valley of Nubia and will cover large districts in the Sudan.

It is estimated that this gigantic lake will be able to irrigate nearly eight million acres of land, thus doubling the cultivatable land of Egypt. In addition, more than half-a-million acres of rice fields will receive its water to make the wet mud that young rice needs to mature in.

As if this were not enough, immense power will be derived from the Dam electrical scheme. But perhaps most important of all, the supply of water will be constant, and the ruinous floods that have haunted Egyptian history will be a nightmare of the past. The immensity of the vision that conceived the High Dam commands our respect and admiration.

In basic economics, the creation and execution of some such scheme as the High Dam was an absolute necessity if Egyptian standards of living were to rise instead of decline. A century ago the country's population was under three million. To-day it numbers well over twenty million people. Moreover, the yearly rate of increase is itself increasing—a kind of compound interest in population—which means that the nation must increase her output by drastic measures calculated to take effect in the lifetime of Egyptians now living.

Over a century ago Mohammed Ali built the Lelata barrage; and the Asnuit, Isna and Naj Hammadi irrigation barrages have carried on the work which that great man initiated. But Egypt must not only distribute the Nile waters to her advantage, she must save them, store them, to make reservoirs of water available when needed and avoid the Nile fluctuations. This she can only do in co-operation with other users of the Nile waters—the Sudan, Ethiopia and the Uganda Governments in particular.

International agreements have long governed the use and diversion of Nile waters, and these agreements—effective and easily operated as long as Britain was the single paramount power involved—recognized that Egypt had a primary interest in the waters of the Nile. The Anglo-Ethiopian Agreement of 1902 safeguarded Egyptian interests held in common with Abyssinia, while an agreement signed by Lord Lloyd, at that time British High Commissioner in Cairo, and the Egyptian Premier, regulates Egyptian-Sudan interests in the Nile waters.

The British Sudan has been superseded by the Sudanese Republic. The Nile capacity of over eighty milliard tons in volume, only fifty milliard of which were used (evaporation and the sea consuming the balance), was apportioned in the ratio of forty-eight to Egypt, only four going to the Sudan. Understandably, the new Sudanese authorities would like a revision of these figures. The Sudan itself is a waxing power politically and economically. At the same time the Sudanese authorities realize that the Egyptian Government cannot be expected to undertake the High Dam project without Sudanese co-operation and support.

Important and profitable discussions have recently taken place in Cairo between the Egyptian and Sudanese authorities on the points involved. Agreement has been found difficult, but it is imperative and will, in time, be achieved.

Alternative plans to the Aswan High Dam have been advanced, but as the World Bank has approved the High Dam project[1] we may take it that it is this plan, modified by the exigencies of practical engineering, that will go through. Over 300 miles of the Nile in Egypt and about half that distance in the Sudan will be flooded. The town of Wadi Halfa will disappear. And some 40,000 Sudanese and other inhabitants will have to be moved, resettled and re-housed. It is strange how the thread of huge works, majestically conceived and heroically accomplished, perpetuates in Egyptian history.

In spite of the immensity of the difficulties we may take it that from the World Bank, from Britain, and from America, ample finance for the High Dam will, eventually, be forthcoming,[1] and that agreement between the Egyptian, the Sudanese and the Uganda Governments will be reached.

Of great importance to antiquaries, but likely to be swept aside as the High Dam becomes a practical reality, is the very large area of land which will never be seen again, having become the bed of the Dam lake.

The vast flooding will also create the most pressing personal problems for the population of Wadi Halfa. Petitions are continually

[1] The Bankers, following the politicians, have now withdrawn their promise of support. The Egyptian Government is carrying on the project alone.

being sent to the Sudanese authorities in Khartoum asking that the High Dam scheme should be scrapped in favour of a plan to build a number of smaller dams which, the Sudanese say, would spread the benefits of the works more evenly and avoid the immense evaporation which would constantly rob the High Dam lake of its water, situated, as it is, in one of the hottest and driest places in Egypt or the Sudan. Wadi Halfa is a transit town of paddle steamers and merchandising. It is an air link for British planes flying north and south. If the population were moved it would probably have to be moved to the northern tip of the new reservoir which would become the point of ingress and egress at the junction of Egypt and the Sudan. There the inhabitants might be able to employ the crafts and skills which they now use. But opposition to the High Dam scheme is sincere and deep in the little town, formerly the seat of a British provincial Governor, and still retaining some it its neat, fastidious air—and an Anglican church where services are no longer held, as they formerly were, every Sunday. When Wadi Halfa disappears, engulfed by the warm, strong waters of the Nile, we can say good-bye to an era, as well as to an obscure Egyptian town.

Far up and down the bank, on either side, the little Nubian villages, with their characteristic rectangular lines, will have to go, with the Temple of Abu Simbel, the masterpiece of Rameses II, cut in the face of the rock. There is no way to save it. The temple, and all the other ruins of interest and importance in the land marked for inundation, are being carefully surveyed by the Egyptian Antiquities service. They are also being drawn and photographed and minutely described and noted. So history will be able to refer to this heritage, which will live on only in the files of the Cairo Museums.

Unesco is co-operating with the Egyptian Government in the compilation of a complete survey of ancient monuments which may be covered by water when the proposed Dam is built.

Professor J. Cerny, the Egyptologist, of Queen's College, Oxford, has joined experts from Italy and America who have started exploratory research in the area of Abou Simbel.

Further archaeological expeditions are planned for this year to ensure that a complete study, including photographic records of the monuments and the evidence they offer of the art and civilization of ancient Egypt can be made before it is too late.

There is a strong body of opinion, both in America and Britain, which regards the High Dam scheme with disfavour. They say that there are some hundreds of miles above the High Dam site where the river is consistently many metres below its ancient levels and where, in consequence, vast areas of potentially fertile land have been abandoned. It is urged that a series of much smaller dams at each of the suitable cataracts would not only store immense quantities of water, but would enable great tracts of land to be reclaimed and re-opened. It would also, by the provision of locks, enable the Nile to be navigable at all seasons of the year up to and beyond Khartoum, with great commercial advantage to Egypt and the Sudan.

But Colonel Nasser has set his heart on the High Dam. If it is built, as now seems likely, the new Government of Egypt, driven on by the irrepressible energy of the Prime Minister, will have added another wonder to the world. Nasser will have left a greater monument than the Pharaohs.

CHAPTER ELEVEN

THE ARMED FORCES

THE Army is, of course, now the number one force in Egypt. It is riding on the crest of a wave of political power and commands the resources of the nation. It is militant, intensely proud, and sensitive, but can it fight? In London I was assured that the fighting qualities of the Egyptian soldier were no better than they had ever been. But General Martin, the able and astute military correspondent of the *Daily Telegraph*, took a different view. I listened to him talk in his office on the third floor of the *Daily Telegraph* building in Fleet Street.

"I think you will find that the morale of the non-commissioned ranks has greatly improved. The German instructors have been largely responsible for this. As for the officers they, of course, as comrades of Nasser, are on top of the world—and our reports show that the large quantities of planes and armour recently imported from the Iron Curtain countries are first rate. The Egyptians have mastered the techniques of the new weapons, though some newspapers have said that this has not yet been accomplished. Yes, I think you are going to find the Egyptian Army a waxing power—and much more efficient that it has ever been."

So I was prepared, when I got to Cairo, to find a live and energetic Army and Air Force. The Egyptian Navy is, of course, in its infancy and can be left out of this discussion as being little more—at present—than coastal and Customs control.

If this is the picture now, we only have to go back a little more than a century to trace the quaint and inauspicious beginnings of the modern Egyptian Army. Since its history has a very direct bearing on the present Army attitude, and is interesting in itself, it is worth while retracing our steps to 1841 during the reign of Mahomet Aly, the founder of the dynasty that ended with King Farouk.

In the Hatti-Sherif of the 13th February, 1841, which the Ottoman Sultan addressed to Mahomet Aly on his acceptance of the conditions imposed by the Sublime Porte, the following was textually included about the Egyptian Army:

"In peace time, 18,000 troops being sufficient for the interior security of Egypt, this number should not be increased. However, as the land and sea forces of Egypt are kept for the service of the Sublime Porte just as the other forces of the Empire, Egypt may, in war time, increase the number of her army by appropriate proportions."

The Hatti-Sherif added:

"According to the new military service system which we have adopted throughout our Empire, the soldiers, after serving for five years, should be replaced by new recruits; this same system will be followed in Egypt. Thus, 20,000 men will be chosen among the latest recruits of the Egyptian troops to begin the new service, out of whom 18,000 men will be kept in Egypt and 2,000 sent here for their training.

"The fifth of these 20,000 men having to be replaced each year, 4,000 recruits will be annually enlisted in Egypt, according to the method prescribed by military regulations by means of drawing of lots, and proceeding with all humanity, fairness and requisite impartiality, 3,600 of these recruits will remain in the country and 400 sent here. The soldiers who complete their training either in Egypt or here will return to their homes and will not be recalled.

"Although the climate of Egypt," continued the Hatti-Sherif, "may demand a difference in the material of uniforms, the style, however, of their uniforms, as well as their decorations and flags, will not be in any way different from those used by other troops of our Sublime Porte. Also, the uniforms and decorations of the officers, sailors and soldiers of the Egyptian Navy, as well as the colours of the vessels, will be the same as these.

"The appointment of the officers of land and sea forces, up to and including the grade of Kol-aghasi (Major), will belong to the Egyptian Government. Higher ranks shall be conferred by us.

"Henceforth, it will not be permissible for the Viceroy of Egypt to build warships without the explicit permission of our Sublime Porte."

In the Firman of investiture of the Khedive Ismail, dated the 8th June, 1873, there was no mention of the Army. But in the one handed to Khedive Tewfik on the 7th August, 1879, only the first paragraph of the above-mentioned Hatti-Sherif was textually reproduced—with this difference, however, that there was no longer the need to send 2,000 men to Constantinople and the total strength of the Egyptian forces was reduced to 18,000 men "for the interior protection of Egypt." It was, however, mentioned that the Egyptian Government would have the right directly to confer higher ranks to officers of land and sea forces up to and including that of Colonel, instead of Kol-aghasi (Major), as was mentioned in the Hatti-Sherif of the 13th February 1841. The Firman of 1892 handed to Khedive Abbas II was the last delivered by the Sultan to the Khedives of Egypt, the Ottoman suzerainty having been abolished following the participation of Turkey in World War I. But the Firman of investiture of Abbass II contained exactly the same text as that of the Firman of Khedive Ismail concerning the Army, that is, 18,000 soldiers, and the right to grant officers' commissions up to and including the rank of Colonel. It is clear that this limitation was in Britain's favour because, since 1882, she occupied the country and was naturally not anxious to reinforce the small Army. On the contrary, she found in it a guarantee against mutiny. Moreover, these 18,000 men did not join active military service. Some were sent to the Sudan and some formed the Khedivial Guard, later known as the Royal Body-Guard. Better dressed and equipped than the rest of the Army, its principal rôle consisted in ceremonial parades, under certain circumstances—accompanying the king in his journeys, and on national holidays—and participating in spectacular reviews.

From 1882, the Commander-in-Chief of the Army—the Sirdar—was always an Englishman surrounded by a general staff of British officers.

One should add here, incidentally, that the Sirdar held the same role with the Egyptian Armed Forces as that which the British Advisers held with the Ministers. His counsels were orders.

Khedive Abbass II paid dearly for it when, fresh from the Theresianum of Vienna where he was educated, he acted as Supreme Commander of the Armed Forces. He therefore went to Upper Egypt, where manœuvres were taking place. While reviewing the troops, he took the liberty of making some remarks at which Kitchener took umbrage, and a serious crisis took place. Abbass II had to make an apology to his subordinate, the irascible Sirdar.

Should the act of violence be also recalled which, in 1924, followed the deplorable murder of Sir Lee Stack? The British authorities found it a good opportunity to make out of an isolated crime almost a *casus belli*, and demand of the Egyptian Government, among other extremely severe sanctions, the immediate recall of Egyptian forces in the Sudan. It was not, however, an easy thing. Egyptian officers and soldiers stationed at Khartoum, amongst whom there were also some Sudanese, refused to obey orders emanating from the Governor-General of the Sudan in his capacity as Chief of Staff. There were armed clashes in which Egyptian and Sudanese officers joined. Nothing short of a special and direct order from the King ordering them to submit could calm them. . . .

In fact, even after the conclusion of the 1936 Treaty, according to the terms of which a mission of British officers should be engaged for the proper training of the Army, this commission carried out its functions, but later the Egyptian Government decided to dispense with their services.

However, as soon as the Council of the Revolution was in power, its principal effort was to improve the state of the Army, fill in its gaps after the sad experience acquired in Palestine. The Council increased its number, gave it modern weapons, raised the pay of the troops, improved their clothing, abolished the service of ordnances and infused in it a feeling of greater dignity; they secured new weapons, called in foreign though conscientious and devoted instructors, and, in a short time, made of the young Egyptian Army a force to be reckoned with, completely different, both morally and materially, from what it used to be under the Occupation régime. Since compulsory military service has been introduced, educated elements have joined its ranks and contributed much to raising its intellectual standard. The Army is capable of defending the country or of resisting any eventual danger of aggression by Israel. Furthermore, while in the past the civil and military authorities were kept, so to speak, in water-tight compartments, they are to-day united.

The Great Pyramid of Cheops and the Sphinx at Guizeh, Cairo

President Nasser and General Abdel Hakim Amer, Chief of Staff of the Egyptian Army

Egyptian women as National Guards

Moreover, other reforms have been realized in the Army. Here are a few examples:

1. Technical research has been reorganized. It is well known that this section is responsible for the specification of weapons.

2. A new section has been created for the technical inspection of war material. It is in charge of the examination and reception of weapons, munitions and material included in a contract.

3. An agreement has been concluded with the Ministry of Commerce and Industry with a view to creating in Egypt a large factory for the manufacture of motor-car tyres, and another one for the manufacture of batteries necessary for the Army. A third factory will produce military parachutes, which have already proved a success, as practical tests having shown that the parachutes manufactured locally are of the very best quality and are second to none either in quality or solidity, compared with those imported from abroad.

4. Factories for the production of light arms and ammunition have already started to operate, under the control of foreign technicians, until Egyptian personnel able to replace them is trained.

5. Special courses have been instituted with a view to improving the technical knowledge of non-commissioned officers and men so that they may follow the progress of military arts in other countries and be able to assume the responsibilities which the new régime has imposed on them.

With this intention, technical missions have been sent to East and West to follow closely the changes which are taking place in military science and armament. There are missions in the United States, India, Pakistan and Turkey.

A large number of Egyptian officers have also been sent to military academies with a view to completing their studies.

6. A series of lectures has been organized at the Armed Forces' Club. They are given by leading men of thought, letters and science.

7. Particular attention is given to raising the standard of non-commissioned officers, who are the backbone of the army. A new generation of non-commissioned officers with adequate technical knowledge will shortly be available. Some of them have already been admitted to the Army as volunteers and are receiving military training under a determined programme.

It is also known that the private soldier is not neglected. His pay has been raised, particularly if he is married, and his clothing has been improved. If he is illiterate, he is taught to read and write. He gets proper treatment when sick. His food is more abundant and of better quality. He sleeps on a comfortable bed. Better still, the new law on compulsory military service stipulates that the civil servant or the employee of a private company who is called to serve with the colours has the right to return to his old post at the time of his discharge from the Army. As for the recruits who are unemployed when they join the Army, a special service has been instituted for the purpose of finding employment for them on their discharge. Many of them have already been employed in private companies. Even disabled men have been able to find suitable jobs.

Briefly, it can be said that the Egyptian Army has, under the new régime, made considerable progress in every field. Nothing can prove this better than the frequent manœuvres which it has accomplished with remarkable success, a fact which has often been expressed by foreign military attachés who attend manœuvres.

Apart from the Army proper, the Government has adopted the National Guard system to mobilize Egyptian youth, both young men and women, in the national interest.

The regular forces of the Army are now reinforced by a National Guard. The creation of the National Guard was the outcome of a general feeling that Egypt's youth should take active part in their country's liberation and defence.

When the 23rd July, 1952, Revolution took place and succeeded in putting an end to monarchy and feudalism, it was realized that the moment was appropriate for Egypt to adopt the National Guard system which rendered the youth in several other countries ready to serve in any emergency. Hence the decision to form the National Guard in Egypt.

It was pointed out in this connection that, by intensive military training, the youth of Egypt would play an outstanding rôle in the moulding of their country's future. In fact, the National Guard is a new milestone in Egypt's history and has marked the end of the period when work for the Fatherland was assessed by loud but empty applause.

The law constituting the National Guard was promulgated on 15th October, 1953. On that occasion, Major Kameleddin Hussein delivered a speech in which he said that war in this atomic age was no longer between one army and another, but that it was rather the will of one nation pitted against that of another. Nations, he added, no longer confined their efforts to the training of their regular armies for action in the battlefield, but also made provisions to safeguard the rear of their forces by means of well-trained formations who would also serve for purposes of civil defence.

It was therefore deemed imperative, he added, that the country's youth should be invited to volunteer for this national service with a view to creating an auxiliary force which would assist the regular Army in the task of national defence.

The National Guard is an auxiliary force belonging to the War Ministry.

It consists of regional units, each one under a commanding officer to be appointed by the Commander-in-Chief of the Egyptian Armed Forces, and is entirely formed of volunteers who must be of Egyptian nationality, not under seventeen or over forty, medically fit and of good character. The National Guard movement, as well as being a useful auxiliary force, typifies the official of the new Egypt.

In order to understand how proud the Egyptians are of the resurrection of their armed forces, I reproduce a résumé of the speech made by the Commander-in-Chief, Major-General Abdel Hakim Amer, in Republican Square, reporting on the armed forces to the nation on the anniversary of the Revolution.

The language is a little more flowery than American or British Commanding Officers are wont to use when they can be persuaded to speak at all, but I have left the text as it is, for it indicates the good opinion which the Egyptian Army now has of itself and warlike action.

"In the name of the Revolution and in the name of Liberty I submit to you to-day the balance sheet covering the past two years of trusteeship, during which I have been in charge of the Armed Services, the Army, the Navy and the Air Force.

"Despite the increasingly heavy responsibilities of our Armed Forces, our men have discharged their sacred duties with patience, fortitude and determination, enforcing law and order under the critical eye of Egypt's enemies.

"Our main task lay in consolidating our position, not only on the home front, but also on the wider field of international relations. In this, as in other vital matters, our men were always prepared for the fray.

"Should zero hour come, however, our forces will not stand isolated, nor will they fight alone on the battlefield. They will be staunchly supported by the whole nation in arms, fighting alongside with them shoulder to shoulder, in the units of the National Guard, which are now 60,000 strong, or with the crack 3,000 commandos, who are eagerly looking forward to the day of sacrifice.

"On that day the whole nation will be on the move. Taking the lead in battle array our fighting services will be operating in accordance with long-prepared plans that have taken months of careful study to evolve, in anticipation of the most exacting requirements of modern warfare.

"Regarding the Army formations and units, parachute troops have come into being and these will be organized and strengthened to constitute the mainstay of our striking force.

"Plans have been made for the reorganization of the infantry in the light of recent experiments and, before this year is out, the fire-power of our divisions will be considerably increased by new equipment.

"Closer co-operation between our ground and air forces is being established and a tactical air command has been set up to provide adequate cover in the field.

"Meanwhile the Navy has been thoroughly reorganized on the assumption that its main task will be the defence of our territorial waters and our advanced bases.

"As for armaments, we have succeeded in supplying all our units with medium and light weapons of the up-to-date models, despite all sorts of obstacles placed in our way by our foes, and it is hoped that more war material will be made available in the not-too-distant future.

"Great quantities of ammunition, jet bombers and essential strategic raw materials have been imported, while orders have been placed with local manufacturers for the production of rockets, shells, mines and spare parts. And while we are already producing here in Egypt our own training planes, known as the 'Republic', the coming months will witness an uninterrupted stream of arms and ammunition pouring out from our own war factories, the creation of which had always been considered, until July 1952, as the fantastic dream of a heat-oppressed imagination.

"In order to avoid the calamities which befell the Egyptian forces fighting in Palestine we have set up a Technical Inspection Corps, whose duty it is to test every weapon supplied to our men and to supervise the fulfilment of Army contracts. Only our most efficient officers and best-qualified experts are recruited for this corps.

"With the growing importance of technique in modern warfare we have had to cater for the scientific training of our officers and men. In addition to the Higher Institute of Strategy, which is designed to ensure a regular supply of competent staff officers, an Academy for Senior Flying Officers was recently opened and soon a training centre for N.C.O.s will be inaugurated.

"This is the first stage of a wider educational programme which is intended to embrace every field of Army activity—notably trades and crafts—so that the production capacity of every man is gradually increased.

"In pursuance of the noble aims of the Revolution, we have spared no efforts to raise the general standard of living of the N.C.O.s and men. Laws have been issued to deal with such questions as family allowances to married recruits, pensions to the next-of-kin of deceased soldiers, insurance and savings schemes, hospitals and convalescent homes, as well as service indemnities to help the demobbed.

"Other projects under examination include notably a large-scale scheme to provide comfortable living-quarters for our men stationed outside the main cities. They will be accommodated in large barracks with sports fields, swimming pools, educational, social and welfare centres.

"Being an integral part of the nation, the Armed Forces have contributed in no small share in every new industrial scheme intended to achieve economic self-sufficiency. It is in this spirit they have actively promoted the car spare-parts local industry, the tyre and rubber industry, the dry battery factory and the dockyard project for the building of warships and an Egyptian merchant fleet.

"Beyond our shores and territorial boundaries technical assistance has been extended by our armed forces to the Sudan and the member States of the Arab League, certain African countries, in order to weave stronger bonds of friendship between those nations and the Egyptian people.

"Besides supplying these nations with arms and ammunition, we have despatched military missions there to replace the foreign advisers who were in charge of their Army training, while in other cases, their army cadets were put under training in our own academy.

"Military co-operation with the Arab nations has been markedly efficient in the laying down of a joint defence plan to repulse aggression against the member States of the Arab League.

"In the wider pattern of international relations, great prestige has been earned by our armed forces in several capitals of the world, especially in Asia, Europe and America. The scope of our military representation abroad has been widely extended; friendly Asian and South-European nations have invited us to send official military missions and the Egyptian Navy has made successful courtesy visits to many Mediterranean ports, Red Sea ports, India and Pakistan.

"It is with this proud record in hand that I introduce the armed forces to the nation in the name of the Revolution."

These are the official plans and thoughts of the High Command. But what of the officers themselves? And what of their equipment? Is Egypt now a fighting nation to be reckoned with, or, in the event of war—with Israel for example—is she going to suffer again the humiliating defeat of the Palestine campaign, being beaten by young Israelis whose country had hardly time to organize the most simple and rudimentary armed forces?

I received some material on this subject which I do not think it fair to publish until my hosts the Egyptians see fit to do so, but Lt.-General H. G. Martin has been kind enough to supply me with this expert assessment of Egyptian and Israeli military strength:

"The British Government's reluctance to publish details of the arms supplied to Egypt and Israel during the past year or so has made it difficult to form an opinion on how far Arab and Israeli claims and counter-claims for arms are justified.

"But, by cross-checking reports from various sources, it is now possible to make a valid comparison. When in the autumn of 1954 Britain lifted the embargo on the supply of arms to Egypt, the Egyptian Army contained two infantry divisions and an armoured division. It consisted of the following major units:

"Seven infantry brigades and a machine-gun brigade; two armoured regiments, equipped with Shermans; a reconnaissance regiment; four field artillery regiments, armed with 25-pounders, and one armed with 105 mms.; two anti-aircraft brigades armed with 3·7-in. and 40-mm. guns; one coast defence brigade; a complement of engineers and signals.

"In addition, there were half a dozen Centurion tanks of early mark, unallotted to regiments.

"At the same time, the Egyptian Air Force consisted of one nominal squadron of each of the following: Meteors, Vampires, Dakotas, Halifaxes, Lancasters, Spitfires, Hawker Furies, and Commando transports. The actual strength of these squadrons varied with the spare parts situation.

"The Egyptian Navy consisted of two Hunt Class destroyers, four frigates, two corvettes, seven mine-sweepers, and six M.T.B.s.

"Now, a year later, Israeli reports put the tank strength of the Egyptian Army as high as 200 to 300 Shermans. The Egyptians have also placed an order with us for 64 Centurions, of which 32 have been delivered.

"The Marquess of Reading, Minister of State, Foreign Office, stated on Wednesday that no tanks had been delivered to Egypt since mid-August, and that no more were due for delivery. It would be interesting to learn what has happened to the other 32.

"Israeli reports put Egypt's aircraft strength now as high as 82 Meteors, Vampires and Venoms, with 34 more on order.

"As to the future, according to reports from the United States, Skoda is to supply Egypt with the following at one-fifth to one-tenth market price: 200 MIG 15 fighters, a number of 11-28s jet bombers, 100 tanks, 6 submarines, and large quantities of artillery. Some of the fighters and bombers, it appears, have already been delivered.

"Against all this, the Israeli forces consist of a covering force of 3 brigade groups, expandable to 16 on mobilization. The weapons in use are 25-pounders and 76 mm. Krupp field-guns, multiple rocket launchers, 52 mm., 81 mm. and 120 mm. mortars, 7·92-mm. F.N. light machine guns, Veza medium machine guns and Mauser rifles.

"Israel's efficient 'Military Industries' manufacture small arms and ammunition.

"Most of the Israeli tanks are reconditioned Shermans. But the French have now supplied some AMX tank destroyers, armed with 75-mm. high-velocity guns.

"The Air Force consists of one squadron of Meteors, one training and one operational squadron of Mosquitoes, three B-17 Flying

Fortresses, three Catalinas and some German war-time aircraft. Some French Mystere fighters are on order.

"The British Government has refuted Col. Nasser's accusation that it has recently supplied Israel with 50 Mustangs and 100 Shermans and 15 Churchill tanks. When the Israelis placed an order with Britain for 30 Centurion tanks, we offered 6 only, and subsequently cancelled that offer.

"According to *Jane's Fighting Ships*, the Israeli Navy consists of 2 former British destroyers, 5 frigates and a number of M.T.B.s.

"There is nothing in the above comparison to justify Col. Nasser in his recourse to Skoda for arms."

It would not be fair to end a chapter on the Egyptian Army without saying that the Egyptian Army officer is often a most presentable and attractive person. The long British association with the Egyptian Army has at least left behind a tradition of personal smartness, good manners and humour. Of all the classes I met in Egypt I found the Army officers the most congenial.

The martial tradition in Egypt goes back further than in most countries, and the officers and men of the Egyptian Army to-day feel that they are the direct inheritors of a proud and valiant history.

CHAPTER TWELVE

THE YOUNGER GENERATION

I WAS anxious, during my stay in Egypt, to get in touch with young Egyptian boys and girls and to find out what impact the Revolution had made on them. The wealthy merchants, the Army Officers in power, even the elder fellaheen would soon be a previous generation. If there was something fine and invigorating to be got from the Revolution, it was the school children and the university students who, largely, would have to develop it. It is exceptionally difficult for a foreigner to penetrate the heart and mind of young Arabs, but I tried, and, as a result, I formed some interesting impressions.

As soon as one starts to talk to them one realizes that their religion, and the social habit that has grown up around it, has had a permanent influence on their manners, mode of thought, and on their way of life. I found the young men suspicious, anti-European, adroit, and well-versed in the ways and means by which they might enrich themselves. It is not an altogether attractive picture, but there were delightful exceptions to it. The disdain of foreigners which Egyptians youth, in spite of their outward politeness, seem to harbour as something precious, goes back, I am convinced, to the Founder of their Faith. All that has happened since has been less penetrating, less permanent. Centuries of absolute monarchy left its impression. The French and British occupation only added fuel to a fire that was already burning. Mohammed himself set the pattern, which persists to this day.

This description of Mohammed, by George Sale, I find fascinating in its combination of realism, adroitness and courage.

"Mohammed came into the world under some disadvantages, which he soon surmounted. His father Abd'allah was a younger son of Abd'almotalleb, and dying very young and in his father's life-time, left his widow and infant son in very mean circumstances; his whole substance consisting but of five camels and one Ethiopian she-slave. Abd'almotalleb was therefore obliged to take care of his grand-child Mohammed, which he not only did during his life, but at his death enjoined his eldest son Abu Taleb, who was brother to Ad'allah by the same mother, to provide for him for the future; which he very affectionately did, and instructed him in the business of a merchant, which he followed; and to that end he took him with him into Syria when he was but thirteen, and afterwards recommended him to Khadijah, a noble and rich widow, for her factor, in whose service he behaved himself so well that, by making him her husband, she soon raised him to an equality with the richest in Mecca.

"It is scarce to be doubted but that Mohammed had a violent desire of being reckoned an extraordinary person, which he could attain to by no means more effectually than as a messenger sent by God, to inform mankind of His Will. This might be at first his utmost ambition, and had his fellow-citizens treated him less injuriously and not obliged him by their persecutions to seek refuge elsewhere, and to take up arms against them in his own defence, he had perhaps continued a private person, and contented himself with the veneration and respect due to his prophetical office; but being once got at the head of a little Army, and encouraged by success, it is no wonder if he raised his thought to attempt what had never before entered into his imagination."

The secretive, sometimes selfish character of the young Egyptian man is a constant trial to the leaders of the Revolution who, apparently, would wish him to be as straight and as simple a supporter as any American youth is of his President and country. The battle for the hearts and minds of the school and university student has only just begun. I was assured that great strides had already been made but, when I spoke to individuals, again and again I would come up against what appeared to be insularity of outlook, off-set by exaggerated ideas of Egyptian importance, detestation of foreigners and all their ways—and a wily, subtle, calculating approach to even the simplest problems of life.

The girls appear to be much less complex. Up to the age of fifteen they are, for the most part, obedient, faithful, demure and charming. Before they are sixteen, sex has entered their lives and they are apt to concentrate on it to the exclusion of other matters which seem to them, more and more unimportant. Here again there were surprising exceptions—girls who could compare in every way with Western women in their upbringing, knowledge and *savoir faire*. But that was not the general picture.

Polygamy is now little practised in Egypt; but it is, of course, legal, and involves no social stigma though, in Government circles, it is looked upon as a little old-fashioned. As I talked to young Egyptian women, not yet married, I felt that here, too, their attitude towards life and love—which to them are one—goes back to the Koran and to the Prophet's attitude towards his own women, and to women in general.

George Sale writes of Mohammed and women with charming detachment:

"That Mohammed was, as the Arabs are by complexion, a great lover of women, we are assured by his own confessions; and he is constantly upbraided with it by the controversial writers, who fail not to urge the number of women with whom he had to do as a demonstrative argument of his sensuality, which they think sufficiently proves him to have been a wicked man, and consequently an impostor. But it must be considered that polygamy, though it be forbidden by the Christian religion was, in Mohammed's time frequently practised in Arabia and other parts of the East, and was not counted an immorality, nor was a man the worse esteemed on that account; for which reason Mohammed permitted the plurality of wives, with certain limitations, among his own followers, who argue for the lawfulness of it from several reasons, and particularly from the examples of persons allowed on all hands to have been good men; some of whom have been honoured with the Divine correspondence. The several laws relating to marriages and divorces, and the peculiar privileges granted to Mohammed in his Koran, were almost all taken by him from the Jewish decisions, and therefore he might think those institutions the more just and reasonable, as he found them practised or approved by the professors of a religion which was confessedly of divine origin."

The former humility of the young Egyptian woman, the importance she attaches to sex and finding a husband while she is still very young, was linked with the inferiority of her position from the days of Mohammed until the present day. Another factor may well be that her period of beauty and attraction is still so short. From fifteen to twenty she is often lovely; her eyes dark and lustrous, her figure firm and supple, and her complexion a warm olive that has its own attraction. Then, quite suddenly, she runs to fat, and loses her appeal. Before this happens, she must marry. European girls have another ten or fifteen years in which to make up their minds. The Egyptian girl, with her youthful attraction, feels it of vital importance to secure a husband while men are still attentive to her.

Before the Revolution the attitude of young Egyptian men towards women was extremely realistic. The attitude was: "Women must have men. Given the opportunity they all want love. It is up to us to provide the opportunities as often and as pleasantly as possible." King Farouk was the head of Society and the richer, more educated classes followed him. The young men of Egypt followed and, in the Services, the professions and in commerce, they made women their chief recreation. When the King chose his last Queen she was very young and engaged to a respectable and devoted man. The King did not hesitate to take her. The example was followed by fashionable Egyptian youth.

When the Revolution came, the leaders were faced with young men and women such as I have described and a social pattern of behaviour which was more lax than in some other Near Eastern countries.

Colonel Nasser, a family man of much moral strength and natural rectitude, started at once to try to fit the youth of his nation into a more mature pattern. Up to the present day, he has only touched the outer fringe of the problem, but at least he and his Minister of Education are active in a number of ways.

The problem is being tackled by a new educational system, not yet fully worked out, but with the avowed objects of developing primary education, which extends from six to twelve years of age, through the integration of as large a number of pupils as possible of both sexes into the new scheme of compulsory education; of encouraging pupils to select vocational curricula which give them access to agricultural, industrial and commercial professions following the stage of primary education, in order to help in carrying out large-scale development projects; and of affording equality of opportunity to all Egyptians to attain the highest level of education, either theoretical or practical, compatible with personal inclinations and background.

Nasser realizes that he has to do much more than change the educational pattern in the schools and increase the facilities of the poorer students. Universal compulsory free education is envisaged and is being planned, but the most effective steps so far taken by the Government are their attempts to create a better social life for young people and to protect their health.

The example given by the Duke of Edinburgh in Britain has not escaped the Egyptian leaders, who have embarked on an ambitious scheme of new playing-fields. Up to now, only a small minority of Egyptian boys and girls have played any game at all. The lack of exercise certainly contributed to the early aging of the girls, and to the unfitness of many young men.

The first playground was opened in 1940, but there are now twenty-five first-rate playing-fields. In 1954, a separate body was created to supervise and administer the playgrounds which, until then, had been Government-controlled. An inadequate grant was made by the Government towards playground maintenance. This inadequacy of financial backing seems to be typical of the sums made available for social projects. Still, the Government has made a start. Fifteen new playgrounds are planned for the current year, 1956, and the playgrounds I saw myself were certainly being used to the full for cricket, football and baseball.

In 1953, a General Youths' Club Union was started with sixty-three clubs, which have now increased to nearly four hundred. The Government has taken on the Holiday Camp idea and developed it to suit its own requirements. Two permanent camps were opened in 1954—one at Al-Arish, the other at Ras-el-Barr. Each can house four hundred students. The students usually stay a month, so that the camps cope with twelve batches a year and, incidentally, as a result, are not as hygienic as they should be.

The provision of libraries in the country districts has been backed by the Government. At present the books and periodicals are mainly in Arabic, though a few foreign publications appear. The distribution is through the village clubs. There is a plan for floating mobile libraries but, like many another project in Egypt, it awaits funds.

All these Government endeavours receive general support from such foreigners as have interested themselves in the inner problems of Egypt. But there are two aspects of the Government's general educational policy that are, I think, open to criticism. The first is the stress being laid on vocational training as opposed to general education; the second is the tendency to cut down on English as the second language of the educated Egyptian.

Both these tendencies reflect the attitude of the military leaders of the Revolution who see the urgent need for trained mechanics and technically educated men and women. Such jobs have in the past been largely in foreign hands and the present stress on vocational training is linked up with the natural desire to get all foreigners out as quickly as possible, filling their places with trained Egyptians.

In fact what is most desperately needed in Egypt is a broad, humane education to do away with the narrow, insular prejudices which many people—the young as well as the old—cling to.

The cutting down of the time devoted to learning English is equally short-sighted. For the Egyptians Arabic must be their first tongue and now, for political reasons connected with the Arab League, it is more than ever important, but English is no longer so much a "foreign language" as the international commercial language of the world. More and more, throughout the Arab States, English has supplanted French in all matters that affect trade and commerce. Some of the Far Eastern countries have realized this and, putting their nationalism on one side, have enormously improved their standard of English teaching. But, in Cairo, English is in disfavour—the language of the "hated Imperialists" who, now, at last, are no longer a power in the land.

There are four universities in Egypt: the Al-Azhar University, a shrine of Islamic culture, the Cairo University, formerly called Fuad I University, the Alexandria University, (formerly Farouk I) and the recently founded Ibrahim University. In addition there is the Assiut University which has been described by the authorities as "still in foundation". It is, in fact, a blue-print.

I spent many pleasant hours in the universities, and found the professors charming, if curiously self-centred. But it was the students I was chiefly interested in. I wanted to see how they compared to the men of my own University of Cambridge, or with the products of Yale or Princetown.

I made friends with a young law student, Mustafa, the son of a doctor I had consulted in Cairo. Perhaps because I was an English barrister, and because I recalled my early struggles with legal examinations, I was able to find common ground with Mustafa, and persuade him to tell me what he really thought about life and current events.

We had many conversations, but his answers to my questions were always the same. He was an engaging youth with, I think, some admixture of Sudanese blood. Well-built, he looked less Semitic than most Egyptians. He was frank and often amusing. Our conversations went like this:

Myself: "What foreign nations do you most like and respect?"

Mustafa: "The Germans and the Russians. The Russians have recently helped us to arm when you and the Americans would not supply us. The Germans would have liberated us during the war if Rommel had got through."

Myself: "What foreign nations do you most dislike?"

Mustafa: "The British and the Jews. You have always treated us as inferiors, occupying our country and even breaking agreements with us by stationing a huge army on the Canal instead of the ten thousand men which you agreed to, under the Treaty. The Jews have injured all Arabs by hounding nearly a million Arabs from their homes. The Israel State was created by Britain as a threat to Egypt."

Myself: "Are you glad the Monarchy has been abolished?"

Mustafa: "I don't think the abolition of Monarchy has made a great difference. It is the change of men that counts. We have not reached Democracy yet, or even Committee Rule. We have had one man for centuries. But any one can see that Premier Nasser is a good man and that King Farouk brought our country into contempt!"

Myself: "Do you hate individual Englishmen?"

Mustafa, smiling, replied: "Of course not. But we know that the British are always saying how unreliable and shifty we are, behind our backs. So we don't like them as a race. Besides, their manners are very cold and disagreeable by our standards."

Myself: "Will you marry an Egyptian girl? And when do you expect to marry?"

Mustafa: "Yes, I would not marry a foreigner. If I did I should feel I had a mistress—not a wife. I don't think I'll be able to marry before I'm twenty-five—unless my father helps me a lot."

Myself: "Do you play any games?"

Mustafa: "I play tennis."

(Later I was to learn that Mustafa was something of an 'ace'. About his tennis he was modest and taciturn.)

Myself: "Do you think Egypt has a role to play in the Middle East?"

Mustafa: "Of course she has. We are all Arabs with the same language, religion and blood. But the brains are very largely here in Egypt. Besides, we hold the gate between East and West. Sooner or later Egypt must become the leader of the Arab States. Then we shall be regarded as a great Power—as great as we were in the days of our glory."

Mustafa, in answering my questions, spoke with complete sincerity and spontaneity. He was not trying to impress me. Nor were his answers calculated. They came promptly, reflecting what he really believed. His engaging candour impressed me. Here was a young man of good family, of liberal upbringing, and healthy in mind and body. His detestation of what Britain stands for I found disturbing. I realized it would take great imagination, and a complete change of policies, to reach the young men of Egypt and make them friendly to Britain. It is not impossible, but it will be exceptionally difficult.

I asked Mustafa if he had been impressed by the efforts of the British Council in Cairo. He laughed. "They're pathetic," he said. He complained that no attempt whatever had been made to match the change in Egyptian outlook since final independence.

"We don't want lectures on British poetry," he said. "We don't want your culture crammed down our throats. We have our own culture, three thousand years older than yours! Why don't you tell us about the things you understand? About your motor-racing, your jet-planes and your great expeditions to the Himalayas and the Antarctic? These things would be welcomed here and we would not feel that we were being talked down to and asked to look up to an alien culture. The present British propaganda is drivel, as far as we go. You'd much better save the money and sack these British Council people."

I felt that Mustafa was being unfair to the number of educated and intelligent Englishmen and women who, in the British Council Office, are trying to do a good job. But at least his reaction, which seemed typical, is worth recording. Perhaps we are, after all, on the wrong lines.

One of the difficulties of promoting better education in Egypt in the schools and universities is that Nasser and his associates dis-

Jockeys waiting at the Heliopolis Racing Club

Egyptian women fencing

The Corniche road at Alexandria

trust the professorial type. They certainly express contempt for them. "The pedagogues", Nasser calls them. Adding: "They fawn round me and can say nothing but 'I—I—I——' to insinuate their own personal interests." What the "pedagogues" think of Colonel Nasser is not recorded, but they are certainly obsequious to him in public.

Nasser feels that the vision of the Revolution has not been seen by the university and school teachers; that its boldness and selflessness baffles them.

Colonel Nasser has frequently said that there is no undue Soviet influence in Egypt, and I found little Russian literature, in translation, in the University libraries. I think that Egyptian youth, just now, admires the Soviet Union for "standing up" to the British-American alliance. Russia has never done Egypt any harm. She is a great power. To take an interest in Soviet philosophy and culture is a natural outcome. Nasser does not fear this trend in the least, but regards it as a healthy reaction against British and French cultural predominance.

Nasser has goaded the indolent and often greedy Government doctors into far greater activity, insisting on regular tours to the country districts, and regular submission of disease-figures—which he checks himself by surprise visits from time to time!

He has started a centre for disabled persons and a women's Health Clinic. By intense Government propaganda he is overcoming the fellaheen prejudice against vaccination and inoculation. Nasser is at his best in pressing on with his schemes for Public Health. For such plans directly benefit, in a concrete and practical form, the men and women whom, one cannot doubt, Nasser wishes to help: the common people of Egypt, who have suffered for so long, in silence and in fortitude.

NOTE. The recent visit of Mr. Shepilov, the Soviet Foreign Minister, to Cairo was an acknowledgment of the increased ties of friendship and commerce that link the Soviet Union and the new Egypt.

CHAPTER THIRTEEN

ACHIEVEMENTS, AND THE ROAD AHEAD

When Colonel Nasser and his comrades, having at last finished their day's work, meet to discuss the general situation, they look out on a confused and angry world, and are not dismayed. This is the situation as they see it.

Ultimate power—the ability to do the world irreparable harm, perhaps even to destroy civilization as we know it—is in the hands of three men: the Premier of the Soviet Union, the Prime Minister of Britain, and the President of the United States. Only these men can order the use of thermo-nuclear weapons with a power so devastating that the scientists themselves cannot accurately calculate it.

It is commonly thought that Britain is far behind her rivals in the atomic race. Colonel Nasser does not think so. The Egyptian information is that the Soviet Union have now by far the greatest pile of atom bombs, that Britain leads the field in the manufacture of "cheap" mass-produced weapons, and that the United States leads in guided missiles. But, in atom development, enough is enough, more may be useless. So the Egyptians sum up the matter by saying that any one of these men holds ultimate power.

Nasser himself believes that the peace of the world has been maintained only because the Russians learnt how to manufacture atomic weapons in time. Had they not done so, an attempt to bomb Communism to death was, he thinks, inevitable. If this is so, it involves the strange conclusion that we owe the preservation of peace to the treachery of two or three British and American scientists.

When they look at this grim picture the Egyptians are undismayed, for two reasons. First, they say, the Big Powers are restrained by fear. Small powers are not. During the last five years a tacit understanding has grown up that atomic weapons shall on no account be used in small wars. Only what, by a grim twist of humour, are now called " conventional " weapons may be used. This suits Nasser very well.

There is another factor that the shrewd Egyptians take into account. Each of the Big Three Powers has a different interest. The real idealistic clash is between America and Russia. Britain, loyal ally though she is, has a different interest, imposed by her innate Socialism and by her Commonwealth. She is a middle-of-the-road power by force of circumstances. So the three watch each other like hawks.

In other words, there are two kinds of security: that enjoyed by the Big Three because they are so big, and that enjoyed by States such as Egypt because, in comparison, they are so small. Within this immunity given him by world conditions, Gamal Abdel Nasser feels free to develop his plans and defy any attempt by the Great Powers to regulate his conduct.

He did this very recently at Alexandria. Speaking at a flag-raising ceremony on a number of mine-sweepers and torpedo boats bought under the Czech arms deal he said:

" Egypt can buy arms anywhere. Anyone who tries to stop us will be branded as an enemy of Egypt. We will stand no interference from the Great Powers. The time for orders is past. We are a free country, free to buy arms where we wish in any quantities we may desire."

Referring directly to a Paris meeting of Mr. Dulles, Mr. Selwyn Lloyd and Monsieur Pineau he went on:

"No three countries can decide what should be done in Egypt. We take orders from no one. Let this be understood."

So there it is. Hands off Egypt! And very soon this cry will be extended to ' Hands off the Arab nations.'

For there is no doubt whatever that Nasser's great dream of an Arab Commonwealth is the part of his policy likely to lead to trouble. His dynamic political, social and industrial revolution within Egypt will be followed with sympathy by most nations. When he turns from it to create a new force in world affairs he is running into more open and more dangerous country.

Comparisons have been made in the Western press between Nasser's Arab ambitions and the neutralism of Pandit Nehru. In fact, no two policies could be more dissimilar. Nehru's policy is negative. "India wishes to take no sides in any formation of power *blocs*." He adds that, by remaining aloof, she may be able to perform a service that no participant can accomplish. In the role played by India in the Indo-China War, Nehru saw at least some confirmation of his faith.

Colonel Nasser's plans are not negative. He wishes, by an "international Arab resurgence", to fill the void left in the Near East by Britain and France. And he means to fill it by uniting the Arab peoples. It is commonly said in Britain that the more important Arab States will not accept his leadership. We cannot be too sure of this. Egypt is in many respects a natural Near Eastern leader. The deeper I have penetrated into this matter, the more sure I am that within ten years the natural bonds that tie the Arab States together will develop into some kind of political affiliation. Divided, they are very small fry who can be subjected to economic pressures or won by economic aid. United, they would represent a formidable Near Eastern federation of a hundred million people, great oil wealth, and considerable fighting power. Nasser's golden dream has a practical substance.

One final factor influences Nasser in the bold line he takes with Britain. Egyptians regard both Sir Anthony Eden and Mr. Selwyn Lloyd as mediocrities. They admit that both men have charm, sincerity and experience, but they see them both as cautious, unimaginative men, following, rather than leading, world trends.

While all this is going on, Whitehall is thinking again about Nasser.

Up to now the British attitude has been that Nasser's Arab League policies and Britain's Baghdad Pact were, fundamentally, not in conflict. Both could be said to aim at a preservation of Arab independence, and peace in the Arab area. But now the Foreign Office believes that a real clash exists between the two policies. Britain is going all out to support Iraq and the Northen Tier defence powers.[1] The Foreign Secretary believes that Nasser is out to destroy the Baghdad Pact and replace it with his own all-embracing Arab Federation. How far this switch in emphasis has been brought about by personal antipathies it is difficult to say. But it was a factor.

[1] When Mr. Dulles, and the ailing American President, decided to withdraw from the High Dam, thus provoking the Suez Canal conflict, they incidentally, and indirectly, mortally wounded the Baghdad Pact.

Nasser's offer to stop scheming if the Baghdad Pact was put "on ice" has been rejected, first because the British Government did not believe in Nasser's sincerity, and secondly because the move was regarded as an attempt to wean Iran from the West. Colonel Nasser has always set his heart on winning Persia.

During the London talks with Premier Bulganin, a tentative suggestion was made that Russia should underwrite peace in the Near East. The reply of the Russian Delegation, not revealed, was that peace everywhere concerned them, but that its preservation should not be made a cloak to stifle national aspirations for complete independence. Whatever this may have meant, it is clear that the Soviet Union prefers to play her own game in the Near East. She sees no reason to ally herself openly with the unpopular "Western" powers. Her shadow is enough to restrain their steps, while, at the same time, she smiles encouragingly at the Arab nations, and courts them gently one by one with arms and trade barter.

In pursuing her Arab Commonwealth vision Egypt will fall foul of the Great Powers on at least one question. It is oil. It is a melancholy reflection that neither Britain nor America are really moved except by oil interests. Britons may be murdered abroad with comparative impunity, pensions may be denied British subjects, her Embassies may be insulted, and her Officers sacked. The reaction of Whitehall is always: First: "Do not let us be hasty". Secondly: "Let it go through the usual channels". Two years later the issue is bogged down in paper. But a single complaint from the Oil Firms provokes a scene of excited activity in the British Cabinet. The usual detached and somewhat lethargic men in control spring into the most unwonted activity. The slogan then is: "Let's act and act quickly". Nasser knows this, and it troubles him, but only because of its future implications. At present he knows that he cannot survey the Egyptian oil prospects, far less work the oil if it is found, so he has done his deal with the Anglo-American Oil interests. In the bigger field, Abadan showed that the time had not yet come to turn the foreigners out, but the time will come. The Arab Commonwealth, when formed, will require the ownership of the oil revenue, not a royalty percentage. Then there will be a real clash. At present it pays the Arab States to have their oil resources developed by foreign firms who, incidentally, spend very large sums on prospecting for new wells, as well as working the existing ones. So the great battle for oil looks ahead. Meanwhile the Egyptian Government is friendly with Greece, whose subjects have the largest fleets of oil tankers in the world. One never knows when a friend may be useful.

Nasser's turbulent young régime has met opposition on one more front. He has been roundly accused of opening the door to Communism and Soviet penetration into his own country and that of his allies. His answer, which seems to me a very good one, is that Arab nationalism will never admit Communism. There is no void to be filled. Imperialism and Colonialism, he says, invite Communism because of the oppression and the gulf between the Government and people. I quote his own words which give his argument additional edge and characteristic twist.

" I know that I am accused of opening Egypt, and therefore Africa, to Communism, but it is totally untrue. Russia has been not only in Egypt but all over the world ever since the Battle of Stalingrad in 1942.

" In any case, what is Egypt to do? Egyptian policy is based upon three fundamental considerations—independence; an adequate supply of arms for our defence against Israel; and a sound and prosperous economy based chiefly upon the sale of our cotton. The West no longer buys Egyptian cotton in the quantities it used to, and we have been compelled to look elsewhere; to, for example, Russia, China and Czechoslovakia, which now take a third of all the cotton we produce, in exchange for their own commodities and manufactured goods.

" This is not what we want, but what are we to do?

" Communist propaganda against the West consists of instilling a sense of nationalism into undeveloped peoples who have been colonized in the past. The defence against this is to turn their own weapon against them, in other words to preach nationalism, but with the totally different and opposite objective of making the people of the country proud of it and proud to belong to it.

" The world is waging a new kind of war—the cold war—the war of national psychologies. The only defence is something that makes a people proof against any kind of external pressure, no matter whence it comes, and that defence is nationalism.

" It is certainly possible for Britain and Egypt to be friends, but the first essential is the creation of a feeling of mutual confidence and trust.

"After the signing of the Anglo-Egyptian Treaty in October, 1954, the atmosphere was excellent, and in the December the conference of the Arab Foreign Ministers in Cairo passed a resolution welcoming complete co-operation with the West, subject to no Arab country joining any pact or treaty outside the Arab League.

"A month later you confronted us with the Turko-Iraq Pact, which you have since developed into the Baghdad Pact, a complete change of policy that destroyed all the good feeling that had grown up between us. After that you put pressure upon other Arab States to join it, a policy that would have meant the complete isolation of Egyptians.

"It must be realized that the system of pacts is dead, and that to-day people will not accept any kind of mandate or domination over them. You have got two chief interests in the Middle East—oil and spheres of influence. You will have to sacrifice something, for I do not think you will be able to keep both.

"You produce oil from certain Arab States and pay for it. It is to your mutual advantage that this arrangement should continue, and I do not think that they will ever try to prevent it. But you know what happened at Bahrein the other day, when Mr. Selwyn Lloyd went there. The British adviser to the Sheikh has been there for twenty years, and is looked upon as the representative of British Imperialism just as General Glubb was in Jordan.

"I think that you must change your ideas. If you insist in trying to keep both your oil interests and your spheres of influence, that is to say your military bases, troops and your old imperialistic ideas, it will lead to catastrophe. The only way to secure the goodwill and friendship of the Arab States is to found the defence of the Middle East upon the collective security pact of the Arab League."

At least nobody can say of Colonel Nasser that he has not put his cards on the table. The peace and security of the Arab world he sees secured by the Arabs themselves, not by an overriding foreign alliance.[1] He sees Britain as having forsaken her great imperial role, but as clinging to her old imperial methods of "divide and rule". When one is in Egypt probing these questions, one receives the strong

[1] When Colonel Nasser says that Egypt will not go Communist he is quite sincere. The Communist mentality, founded on envy, and enforced by police rule, makes no appeal to Egyptians.

impression that time and the trend of world development are on the Arab side.

What can be said of the Revolution after four years? Both at home and abroad it has been brilliantly successful. Colonel Nasser can hardly have imagined, in the early dawn of 23rd July, 1952 when power still rested in King Farouk's plump, manicured hands, that he would go so far, so fast.

There have been reverses. The Sudan was the most hurting of these. Nasser was sure that Major Salem had wooed and won the Sudanese. General Neguib, half Sudanese himself, had assured Nasser that all would be well. Then, at the last moment, the fish swam out of reach. The Sudan plumped for full independence—and friendship with Britain, as well as with Egypt. If that decision is due to any one factor, then surely it is due to the British Sudan Civil Service whose tradition was always one of helping the people, and ruling by example.

To this able, devoted and unselfish body of men the British Government and people owe a great debt. One can only hope that Whitehall will not dishonour its obligations towards men who have served Britain so well.

How bitter and personal was the blow to Nasser when the Sudan decided not to throw in her lot with Egypt can be understood only if the background of recent Sudanese history is recalled.

After the occupation of Egypt by the British Forces in 1882, the Sudan question became the object of far-reaching developments.

The fall of Khartoum and General Gordon's assassination, followed by the dervishes' advance towards Wadi Halfa afforded Britain the pretext to stress the necessity of the complete evacuation of Sudanese territory by the Egyptian forces. This made it possible for her later to demand the reconquest of the Sudan by an Egyptian expeditionary force under some British officers and with some British detachments taking part in the campaign. This was not only a heavy financial burden on Egypt but also the cause of a serious loss of life among her sons. After the occupation of Khartoum, the British flag was flown side by side with the Egyptian flag on Government House in the capital of the Sudan.

The 1889 Conventions permitted the British to secure all power in their hands in spite of the condominium.

The Egyptians regard the 1889 Conventions as null and void.

In the first place, they say Egypt was at that time a province belonging to the Ottoman Empire, having no right to conclude with foreign States political agreements which may affect the Ottoman Sultan's sovereignty. This, however, was precisely the motive of the 1899 agreement which Egypt signed or was forced to sign.

Then: The Khedive himself had no right to sign such agreements as, in conformity with the Firman of his investiture in 1892, he was explicitly forbidden to cede any territory with the administration of which he was entrusted.

Finally: In all treaties signed with other Powers, the British Government formally recognized the integrity of the territory of the Ottoman Empire: for instance in the treaty concluded with Austria, Prussia and Russia, the Convention of 15th July, 1841, the collective note of 11th March, 1841, the Memorandum of 15th July, 1841, the Treaty of 30th March, 1856, and the Treaty of Berlin of 1878. The British Government, moreover, recognized the validity of all the Firmans issued to the Khedives. The Sudanese provinces were declared to be "Ottoman" particularly by the Convention of 1884 with the free Congo State. In 1898, it advanced this as an argument during the incident of Fashoda. Thus, until 1924, Britain never ceased to declare on every occasion that she acted in the Sudan in the name and for the account of Egypt.

The condominium was a farce, yet Egypt has invariably given proof of her interest in the Sudan. For over thirty years she bore the expense of the maintenance of the Sudan Defence Force. As for education, Egypt has contributed to its promotion among all classes of the Sudanese people.

The present régime is contemplating the establishment of an Egyptian University at Khartoum as well as several religious institutions.

In the agricultural and industrial fields Egypt has sent experts and technicians to introduce in the Sudan modern methods of agriculture as well as the technique of modern industry.

Egypt has made a free gift to the Sudanese Defence Force of her barracks in the Sudan, coast long-range batteries as well as considerable quantities of arms and war material.

In 1947, an Under-Secretary of State for Sudan Affairs was appointed with offices at the Presidency of the Council of Ministers. The idea was that this official should establish such contact with the

Sudan that he might give advice to the Government on all matters relating to the Sudan.

An arrangement was made with the Bank of Agricultural Credit with a view to placing a considerable amount at the disposal of agricultural enterprises in the Sudan, particularly with regard to the supply of agricultural machinery, implements, selected seeds and fertilizers.

In the cultural field, the present régime gives considerable grants to Sudanese students completing their higher education in Egyptian Universities; each one of these students, now about 5,000 in number, is receiving the sum of £E.8 per month. An additional £E.5 is paid every month to any student who gives proof of diligence and special aptitude.

It was a bitter blow to Nasser when the Sudan, in spite of all this courtesy, turned down union with Egypt.

The struggle for the Sudan goes on; the Egyptian Government has not relinquished its aim to unite the two nations, if not in a single unit, at least by the closest treaty ties. In this aim they are helped by the interdependence of Egypt and the Sudan. The plans for the High Dam have shown again how intimate and intricate these ties are.

Yet the Sudanese, once having tasted independence, are less and less likely to give it up. Their revenue may be small, but their needs also are very modest. Industrialization has not yet reached them. They have no population problem. A proud, simple people, well capable of governing themselves, they will not, in the foreseeable future, become involved in the vast plans, at home and abroad, which Colonel Nasser entertains. For twenty years the new Sudanese politicians can apply themselves to building up their own new economy and political status—and still the task will be unfinished.

As I write these words, the effect from day to day of Cairo Radio and of Arab feeling against Britain is seen in the reports reaching London from abroad. When Lord Lloyd, Parliamentary Under-Secretary of State, left Aden, after telling the people that no immediate changes in the Constitution of Aden could be allowed, this was the scene at the airport.

"Police armed with rifles, batons and metal shields stood by when Lord Lloyd left for Hargeisa, British Somaliland. Riot squads patrolled the six-mile route from Government House. Along the route a crowd of several hundred Arabs had gathered to shout anti-British slogans, and to shake their fists at Lord Lloyd's car."

The report goes on to say that one hundred and thirty tribesmen who had crossed, armed, into East Aden protectorate in three trucks were arrested after R.A.F. Venom Jet Fighters had made dummy runs over the trucks.

There is daily proof that the hot, angry radio of Cairo is getting across to the Arabs wherever they are. Colonel Nasser may have had his reverses, but he is hitting back.

Turmoil throughout the Arab lands. A spirit of angry revolt against the West. Plotting and planning in all the Arab capitals. It is not an attractive picture for Britain. Is there anything she can really do about it?

She can do what the present Government (and presumably the next Labour Government) intend to do, that is, fortify the Baghdad Pact powers with arms and financial succour, while keeping Egypt from war with Israel by the Tripartite threat. Egypt knows that the British plan for intervention in the event of an Israeli war is concrete and immediately practicable. That is one reason why Colonel Nasser continues his propaganda. It is the only peaceful weapon left to him. Moreover, above all, he does not want the British back on the Canal invoking their Treaty rights in case of war. He may be temporarily stymied, but he is not silenced.

An alternative course would be for Britain and America to back the Arab League, fostering the good opinion the Arab leaders already have of themselves, lending them arms in moderation, easing their financial difficulties, exchanging "good-will" visits, turning the Arab League into a friendly, nationalistic movement with powerful friends. The Baghdad Pact powers and the members of the Arab League might well be united in an overall Near Eastern Defence Treaty signed by the Arab leaders themselves. In this way the present rampant Arab nationalism might be guided into useful channels instead of being thwarted and inflamed.

To this proposal there are manifold objections, and it remains to be seen along which lines the future will develop.

As I reach the end of my Cairo visit and the end, too, of my study of Arab affairs that started thirty years ago at Cambridge, I still feel that the reawakening of the Arab nations is the most interesting, and not the least important, development since the world returned to the shaky, nerve-racked peace we now endure.

Over these desert Arab lands with their great life-giving rivers, the flag of Britain and the flag of France flew in assured dominion. It may not be far-fetched to prophesy that in the not too distant future a new flag will fly there. It will be the flag of the Arab Federation: the green crescent flag of a united Islam making the prophet's dream come true.

CHAPTER FOURTEEN

CURTAIN

I HAVE come to an end of my visit—the last of five visits to Egypt in the past twenty-five years—and I have collected a great quantity of material and information, some of which cannot be published. I have been treated with the greatest courtesy, although I made it clear that I was writing an independent account of the new régime in Egypt. I knew, during my entire stay, that in some quarters hostility was felt for Britain as one of the powers-that-be, and that a long struggle for supremacy in the Middle East lay ahead: a struggle between the present dominant Anglo-American interests that control Middle Eastern oil, and the new, rising Arab Federation that would, one day not too distant, do two things. It would try to wipe Israel off the map, and it would try to exterminate Western influence in the Arab countries.[1] Although I knew this, and my hosts knew this, never once during my stay was I treated with suspicion or distrust. Egyptian manners are traditional, and Colonel Nasser's turbulent revolution has not changed them.

On my last day in Egypt, a Friday, I decided to do no more work. Here I had been in Cairo, one of the world's most attractive cities by any standards, and day after day I had worked, finding out more and more of what went on behind the scenes, of the real aims and ambitions of the new Government. I had had no time for pleasure. On my last day I decided to be a tourist, one of the increasing number of people who have recently "discovered" that Egypt is almost as near by air, and less costly for living expenses, than the South of France or Switzerland.

After years of lackadaisical detachment the Egyptian Government, through its Tourist Administration, is at last waking up to the importance of the visitor. American statisticians have opened their eyes by pointing out that world annual expenditure on travel is over 2,500 million dollars. Of these nice, hard, convertible dollars

[1] This was written just before the nationalization of the Suez Canal.

300 million go to Italy ("See Naples and Die!"), 250 million to Britain, and 125 to France. Egypt rakes in a mere 50 million, but there is no doubt at all that this will be doubled when the idea of a holiday in Egypt is really put across not only in Chicago and Birmingham, but in Hamburg and Brussels. At present the reaction of the holiday-maker is to object to an Egyptian holiday on several grounds. Roughly these are: "Much too expensive for us. Too hot. What about the language? Is it healthy? Is it clean?" With so many doubts the Egyptians have a hard time selling their country on the scale they should be able to do.

Yet Egypt, which to-day is both clean and healthy, has something to offer that no other country can approach. Egyptian history, for four thousand years, lives. The ancient Egyptians, as we have seen, had the admirable habit of engraving on stone whatever they wished to hand down to posterity. They also wrote on papyrus with reed pens. Their engravings and their writings, as well as the most lovely works in ceramics, gold and silver, have for centuries been preserved by the desert sand as effectively as if they had been frozen. It is a fabulous accident.

One does not need to be an antiquary or an Egyptologist to be fascinated by the Cairo Museum, where the collection of Egyptian antiquities makes the collections in the British Museum, in the Metropolitan, New York, and in the Louvre, seem small and patchy. The reason, of course, is that whereas foreign museums now have to add to their collections by purchase—a failing channel—the Cairo Museum is constantly fed by current excavations.

It was in 1822 that Champollion first deciphered the Egyptian hieroglyphics that had puzzled the world for centuries. Since then immense strides have been made and the secrets of Egypt's past are for all to read. I went through the museum with an enthusiastic curator. As he talked, I tried to take in the spirit of these fantastic keys to a newly awakened history.

The museum is in the form of a rectangle. In the middle of the south side is the main entrance door. If one turns directly to the left and makes a complete tour of the rectangle, inspecting as one goes the side rooms off the main galleries, one has walked through the ages, and has followed the history of Egypt from its remotest inception until comparatively recent times.

The curator was determined I should miss nothing and, before I had been with him ten minutes, I had no wish to take short-cuts.

This tour, a bird's-eye view, so to speak, begins with the most ancient period recorded in history: the Old Kingdom, which began about 3,200 years before the Christian Era. After the Old Kingdom comes the Middle and then the New Kingdom, this last comprising the 18th, 19th, and 20th Dynasties. With these, we reached the eastern end of the North Gallery, with our first interval between the 18th and the 19th, the Akhnaton Room. In that room, in the centre of the North Gallery, the northern-most part of the museum, are the various objects and memorials belonging to the reign of Amen-hotep IV, the so-called "heretic" King, who attempted, towards the close of the 18th Dynasty, to introduce into Egypt the monotheist worship of the Solar Disc, and who created the style of art called Amarnian, from Tel-el-Amarna, the present site of Akhnaton's capital city. Returning towards the entrance door at the south end of the museum, we went down the East Gallery, with its side rooms, which contain the exhibits of the Rames-side, Sait, Persian, Greco-Roman periods—with a side-glance at the Meroe period and its art—and finally the Nubian Epoch: this completed the round of the ground floor.

For the first time in my life I was excited in a museum. I thanked the curator and he said: "Please tell the people you meet in England about what we have here. We have not been able to reach them effectively. They still think of Egypt as being just sand, the Pyramids, the Sphinx and gully-gully men." I promised.

I love to swim, and everyone I met in Cairo said: "The Gezira Sporting Club pool is the *only* place you can go to. You'll find a large number of British members and visitors. It's quite delightful."

I had not come to Egypt this time to meet my fellow-countrymen, however charming they might be, and experience has taught me that your pleasant suburban housewife, when exported to exotic surroundings, is apt to lose her simple, natural personality. I asked whether I could not swim elsewhere. "But, of course, if you want to." "Where?" "Well, at the swimming pool of the former King Farouk at the Abdine Palace—now sternly called 'Palace of the Republic'." The Egyptian who told me this added, a little apologetically: "It's mainly Egyptians, you know."

In spite of being told that at the palace swimming pool I would meet "mainly Egyptians", I went there and, in surroundings of great beauty, I had a long, quiet swim. There were a few young men and girls sitting round the pool at the small tables under the coloured umbrellas, or stretched out in the sun on what appeared to be canvas camp beds. The girls in the party next to me spoke French, but they were Egyptian. They were very young—not more than sixteen, I should say—but they seemed to manage their young men with experienced femininity.

I asked whether the Egyptian swimmers who had won fame in Europe were trained in this pool, but I was told: "No; they do their training in the early morning at the pool of the National Sporting Club." It is typical of Cairo that there are a multiplicity of fine swimming pools, just as there are good hotels and fine, air-conditioned cinemas. I returned to the Metropolitan to have my last lunch. Simon, the head waiter, with whom I was now on friendly terms (largely, I think, because I understood and appreciated his food and wine) had arranged a lunch that was not on the menu, but which, he knew, I should enjoy. He watched me with a benign eye as I ate my melon, the cold pink trout and the quail. When I had finished, he came up to chat.

"I am sorry you are leaving us. So many Americans and British come here and fail to consult me about food. Sometimes I think they just are not interested. But you, monsieur, are interested in the good things of life. That makes my job much more interesting!"

"I am having two friends to supper this evening. A Mr. Halif and his wife. He works in the Government Office. Perhaps you would be good enough to tell the chef. They have been very kind to me and I would like them to enjoy their dinner." But already Simon was writing suggestions on a card, his lean, dark, young face puckered in serious thought.

As an idea struck him, he smiled: "Leave it to me, monsieur. I think I know exactly what will be appreciated."

If it is true that Britain has the best food in the world, and the worst cooking, I cannot help reflecting that we ourselves are to blame. In the first place, when we visit restaurants—during the week, at any rate—we expect to be served *at once*. This, of course, rules out careful individual preparation and cooking at the start. Then we take what we are given, bad though it may be, instead of returning—with as much commotion as possible—inedible food. And, when we are served with exquisite food nine times out of ten we fail to express our thanks!

In Cairo the epicure as well as the antiquary has a wonderful time.

I spent the afternoon at the races, and came to the conclusion that the withdrawal of the British from Egypt had not helped Cairo racing. I saw six races. Four, as far as I could judge, were straight, but two were so flagrantly "fixed" that I was stunned when objections were firmly overruled, and apparently no action taken against the guilty jockeys. However, I enjoyed it. There is no sight more lovely than thoroughbreds coming on to a course, and the happy flash of the jockeys' silks as they canter to the start. Besides, just before the start of what turned out to be one of the two dubious races, a young Egyptian I had met came up to me and whispered the name of a horse—"Arab Star"—in my ear. I looked at the totalizator indicator. "Arab Star" was an outsider with very few tickets. But here I was a stranger; not for me to ask questions. I reached the totalizator window in time to place a one-pound bet to win. Ten minutes later I was collecting over eighteen Egyptian pounds at the paying-out desk. The cashier smiled. "You are well-informed, sir." I nodded gravely.

Content—and considerably richer—I took the taxi back to the hotel to bath and change. As I sipped a drink in my bedroom, I reflected on what a pleasant day I had had. The evening was to be less healthy but equally enjoyable. Halif and his wife arrived a little before eight. The Egyptian dining-hour is around nine. He had been to school in England and to Cambridge, where we had both been to Trinity Hall. That was the link. His wife had never been outside Egypt except for two weeks she had spent with her husband in Paris and Rome—but she was lovely. She had the traditional Egyptian features, but she had more delicacy than is common. She told me she was twenty-three. I knew her husband must be forty-eight or fifty, but they seemed to enjoy each other's company. He was charming and attentive, and she was gay and full of mischief. She was also beautifully dressed. During the evening, I was to learn that her husband was deeply interested in women's clothes.

"I would much rather have been a *couturier* than a diplomat, but my father would not hear of it."

She wore black. It was simple—a beautifully cut dress with black velvet collar and cuffs. The only relief in colour was gold. She carried a gold evening-bag, which contained her powder-compact, lipstick and cigarette-holder in gold. Her ear-rings were beautifully carved traditional Egyptian designs, each different, but similar in shape. She wore a little hat—or was it a hat? More, I thought, an arrangement of gold-leaf on her black hair. It was the most striking effect I had seen during my stay and, as soon as I met them, I turned to Bey Halif and said: "I think your wife is one of the best-dressed women in the world."

He was delighted. She turned to him and said: "Why do you tell me the English have no eyes for fashion?"

He smiled, then looked at his wife. "All rules, my dear, have their happy exceptions."

Simon gave us a dinner that was so good that we were all guilty of gluttony, and the wine was as good as the food. It would not be true to say that I do not remember the rest of the evening. I do. But it certainly had a golden haze. It was two o'clock before I said "Good night" to my charming friends. The eighteen pounds I had won at the races had been taken with gentle firmness by those wily, polite people who rule over the night-life of Cairo. But we had danced to a fine band in the night club that King Farouk, incognito, used to frequent. We were shown his favourite table. And the band had played everything from "Calypso" to "Rock and Roll". As I dropped my friends at their villa, they stood on the steps waving to me. He was waving his hand, and she was waving a black lace handkerchief with her initials on it embroidered —yes, they really were—in gold thread.

The surprising thing was that next morning there was no reaction. My plane left at ten; and by eight I was out of bed and shaving, and I saw, from the mirror, that the wine and the food had left no trace of over-indulgence. In great good spirits I breakfasted, tipped my way out of the warm embrace of the Metropolitan and made for the airport. There I took leave of the representative of that odd but useful body of men who had watched over me with tender solicitude since my arrival—the Tourist Police.

From the first moment of one's arrival in Egypt these days— ("Welcome to Egypt!" says the aiiport sign)—to the last moments ("*Bon voyage*—and come back soon!")—the Tourist Police are at hand to plan one's itinerary, supply information or settle any dispute one may have with local dragomen or hoteliers. To a visiting Britain or American the idea of being cared for by the police may seem odd, and even repugnant. Yet it works very well.

Egypt—Cairo—has been considerably cleaned up in the last four years. The drug-pedlars and the post-card merchants no longer ply their trade opposite the Central Station. The pavements are not cluttered with prostitutes, as the London pavements are—though single men in Cairo need not be lonely. Yet there is a certain amount of visitor-fleecing still going on. I had my taxi-hire-rate fixed by the Tourist Police, and the price was a third less than the lowest quoted to me privately. Moreover, the taxi was spotless, so was the driver. Only once did I see signs of the old Cairo. A seedy-looking customer pressed into my hand six post-cards of a bestiality that was an outrage if one did not laugh at it. But he moved on very quickly—with his cards—when he saw that I was not a purchaser.

The Tourist Police were still in their dark uniforms—a navy blue. In the summer, they told me, they change into white slacks. Here they were, seeing me off, speeding my passport, with its gratis visa, through the formalities, whisking my two bags through the Customs, by-passing the health authorities. After one has got over the idea of being helped on one's way by the police, I must say the Tourist Police of Cairo—most of whom speak five languages, including English, French and Arabic—are a novel comfort. I always felt that, if any kind of difficulty arose, all I had to do was to summon a member of this remarkable force.

Just eight-and-a-half hours after leaving Cairo, we were circling London Airport, awaiting our turn to land. The sun had been shining as far as Paris, but here was England again wrapped in her dim half-daylight, cold and preoccupied. For a moment I wished more than anything else on earth to return to that enveloping Egyptian sun, the good food, the courtesy and the easy laughter. As soon as I was out of the plane and heard again the cheerful cockney badinage, these disloyal thoughts disappeared. Soon I was in the great city again and, in another half an hour, I was sitting in my garden in Blackheath. The daffodils were over, but the tulips were out in their trim, stately majesty.

Next day I paid my visit to the Foreign Office. Two prematurely aged young men listened gravely to my description of what I had seen, the impression I had formed. They said that I painted a more favourable picture of Egypt under the new régime than most visitors from Britain did. I replied that I had admittedly relied to a great extent on Egyptian information, because I thought it right to do so. I was trying to present Egypt as she is, not as we wish her to be. The young men nodded and smiled. I asked if they knew of an expert on the Egyptian armed forces. I wanted to check with an independent observer the information on the armed forces I had been given in Cairo which, I thought, might be wishful thinking. They suggested I should see General Martin, the military correspondent of the *Daily Telegraph* and the best-informed Englishman on this subject. I rang the general and made an appointment. As I was leaving, the older of the two diplomats said:

"We think, perhaps, our own figures, supplied by our people in Cairo, are not entirely accurate or up-to-date. The general will know as much as anyone."

Again I was indebted to the Foreign Office for being so helpful. I have the distinct impression that, during the last few years, and perhaps more particularly since the adverse press arising out of the Maclean and Burgess affair, the Foreign Office has been awakened to the importance of helpful public contacts at home.

I was back in Britain, but that evening, as I dined for the first time for months in my own house, my thoughts went back to Egypt, and I could hear and feel again the clamour of the Cairo streets. I had brought back with me an impression of a dictator with limitless energy and ambition, backed by comrades who shared his vision. Would the warm, loquacious, sensitive people of the new Egypt ever be friends with the reserved, shrewd people of my own country? Would the past ever be blotted out? I thought that there was a chance the two peoples might come together, but the initiative would have to come from us.

We should have to drop all our prejudices. We should have to forget that we were recently Lords in Egypt. One of our leaders would have to go there and say, quite simply: "Let us be friends."

APPENDICES

APPENDIX ONE

HEADS OF AGREEMENT, SUEZ CANAL BASE

between the Government of the United Kingdom of Great Britain and Northern Ireland and the Egyptian Government [with Annexes, Exchanges of Notes and Agreed Minute]
Cairo, October 19, 1954

The Government of the United Kingdom of Great Britain and Northern Ireland and the Government of the Republic of Egypt,

Desiring to establish Anglo-Egyptian relations on a new basis of mutual understanding and firm friendship,

Have agreed as follows:—

ARTICLE 1

Her Majesty's Forces shall be completely withdrawn from Egyptian territory in accordance with the Schedule set forth in Part A of Annex I within a period of twenty months from the date of signature of the present Agreement.

ARTICLE 2

The Government of the United Kingdom declare that the Treaty of Alliance signed in London on the 26th of August, 1936,[1] with the Agreed Minute, Exchanged Notes, Convention concerning the immunities and privileges enjoyed by the British Forces in Egypt and all other subsidiary agreements, is terminated.

[1] "Treaty Series No. 6 (1937)," Cmd. 5360.

Article 3

Parts of the present Suez Canal Base, which are listed in Appendix A to Annex II, shall be kept in efficient working order and capable of immediate use in accordance with the provisions of Article 4 of the present Agreement. To this end they shall be organized in accordance with the provisions of Annex II.

Article 4

In the event of an armed attack by an outside Power on any country which at the date of signature of the present Agreement is a party to the Treaty of Joint Defence between Arab League States, signed in Cairo on the 13th of April, 1950, or on Turkey, Egypt shall afford to the United Kingdom such facilities as may be necessary in order to place the Base on a war footing and to operate it effectively. These facilities shall include the use of Egyptian ports within the limits of what is strictly indispensable for the above-mentioned purposes.

Article 5

In the event of the return of British Forces to the Suez Canal Base area in accordance with the provisions of Article 4, these forces shall withdraw immediately upon the cessation of the hostilities referred to in that Article.

Article 6

In the event of a threat of an armed attack by an outside Power on any country which at the date of signature of the present Agreement is a party to the Treaty of Joint Defence between Arab League States or on Turkey, there shall be immediate consultation between Egypt and the United Kingdom.

ARTICLE 7

The Government of the Republic of Egypt shall afford over-flying, landing and servicing facilities for notified flights of aircraft under Royal Air Force control. For the clearance of any flights of such aircraft, the Government of the Republic of Egypt shall accord treatment no less favourable than that accorded to the aircraft of any other foreign country with the exception of States parties to the Treaty of Joint Defence between Arab League States. The landing and servicing facilities mentioned above shall be afforded at Egyptian Airfields in the Suez Canal Base area.

ARTICLE 8

The two Contracting Governments recognize that the Suez Maritime Canal, which is an integral part of Egypt, is a waterway economically, commercially, and strategically of international importance, and express the determination to uphold the Convention guaranteeing the freedom of navigation of the Canal signed at Constantinople on the 29th of October, 1888.[1]

ARTICLE 9

(*a*) The United Kingdom is accorded the right to move any British equipment into or out of the Base at its discretion.

(*b*) There shall be no increase above the level of supplies as agreed upon in Part C of Annex II without the consent of the Government of the Republic of Egypt.

[1] Commercial No. 2 (1889).

Article 10

The present Agreement does not affect and shall not be interpreted as affecting in any way the rights and obligations of the parties under the Charter of the Untied Nations.[1]

Article 11

The Annexes and Appendices to the present Agreement shall be considered as an integral part of it.

Article 12

(*a*) The Present Agreement shall remain in force for the period of seven years from the date of its signature.

(*b*) During the last twelve months of that period the two Contracting Governments shall consult together to decide on such arrangements as may be necessary upon the termination of the Agreement.

(*c*) Unless both the Contracting Governments agree upon any extension of the Agreement it shall terminate seven years after the date of signature and the Government of the United Kingdom shall take away or dispose of their property then remaining in the Base.

Article 13

The Present Agreement shall have effect as though it had come into force on the date of signature. Instruments of ratification shall be exchanged in Cairo as soon as possible.

In witness whereof the undersigned, being duly authorized thereto, have signed the present Agreement and have affixed thereto their seals.

[1] "Treaty Series No. 67 (1946)," Cmd. 7015.

Done at Cairo, this nineteenth day of October, 1954, in duplicate, in the English and Arabic languages, both texts being equally authentic.

(L.S.) ANTHONY NUTTING.
(L.S.) RALPH SKRINE STEVENSON.
(L.S.) E. R. BENSON.

(L.S.) GAMAL ABDEL NASSER.
(L.S.) ABDEL HAKIM AMER.
(L.S.) ABDEL LATIF BAGHDADI.
(L.S.) SALAH SALEM.
(L.S.) MAHMOUD FAWZI.

APPENDIX TWO

SUEZ CANAL CONVENTION[1]

Between Great Britain, Germany, Austria-Hungary, Spain, The Netherlands, Russia, and Turkey, respecting the free navigation of the Suez Maritime Canal. Signed at Constantinople. October 29, 1888

Article I

The Suez Maritime Canal shall always be free and open, in time of war as in time of peace, to every vessel of commerce or of war, without distinction of flag.

Consequently, the High Contracting Parties agree not in any way to interfere with the free use of the Canal, in time of war as in time of peace.

The Canal shall never be subjected to the exercise of the right of blockade.

Article II

The High Contracting Parties, recognizing that the Fresh Water Canal is indispensable to the Maritime Canal, take note of the engagements of His Highness the Khedive towards the Universal Suez Canal Company as regards the Fresh Water Canal; which engagements are stipulated in a Convention bearing the date of 18th March, 1863 containing an exposé and four Articles.

They undertake not to interfere in any way with the security of that Canal and its branches, the working of which shall not be exposed to any attempt at obstruction.

[1] The text is complete apart from the preamble, which has been omitted as being of little interest or importance.

Article III

The High Contracting Parties likewise undertake to respect the plant, establishments, buildings, and works of the Maritime Canal and of the Fresh Water Canal.

Article IV

The Maritime Canal remaining open in time of war as a free passage, even to ships of war of belligerents, according to the terms of Article 1 of the present Treaty, the High Contracting Parties agree that no right of war, no act of hostility, nor any act having for its object to obstruct the free navigation of the Canal, shall be committed in the Canal and its ports of access, as well as within a radius of three marine miles from those ports, even though the Ottoman Empire should be one of the belligerent Powers.

Vessels of war of belligerents shall not revictual or take in stores in the Canal and its ports of access, except in so far as may be strictly necessary. The transit of the aforesaid vessels through the Canal shall be effected with the least possible delay, in accordance with the Regulations in force, and without any other intermission than that resulting from the necessities of the service.

Their stay at Port Said and in the roadstead of Suez shall not exceed twenty-four hours, except in case of distress. In such case they shall be bound to leave as soon as possible. An interval of twenty-four hours shall always elapse between the sailing of a belligerent ship from one of the ports of access and the departure of a ship belonging to the hostile Power.

Article V

In time of war belligerent Powers shall not disembark nor embark within the Canal and its ports of access either troops, munitions, or materials of war. But in case of an accidental hindrance in the Canal, men may be embarked or disembarked at the ports of access by detachments not exceeding 1,000 men, with a corresponding amount of war material.

Article VI

Prizes shall be subjected, in all respects, to the same rules as the vessels of war of belligerents.

Article VII

The Powers shall not keep any vessel of war in the waters of the Canal (including Lake Timsah and the Bitter Lakes).

Nevertheless, they may station vessels of war in the ports of access of Port Said and Suez, the number of which shall not exceed two for each Power.

This right shall not be exercised by belligerents.

Article VIII

The Agents in Egypt of the Signatory Powers of the present Treaty shall be charged to watch over its execution. In case of any event threatening the security or the free passage of the Canal, they shall meet on the summons of three of their number under the presidency of their Doyen, in order to proceed to the necessary verifications. They shall inform the Khedival Government of the danger which they may have perceived, in order that that Government may take proper steps to insure the protection and the free use of the Canal. Under any circumstance they shall meet once a year to take note of the due execution of the Treaty.

The last-mentioned meetings shall take place under the presidency of a Special Commissioner nominated for that purpose by the Imperial Ottoman Government. A Commissioner of the Khedive may also take part in the meeting, and may preside over it in case of the absence of the Ottoman Commissioner.

They shall especially demand the suppression of any work or the dispersion of any assemblage on either bank of the Canal, the object or effect of which might be to interfere with the liberty and the entire security of the navigation.

Article IX

The Egyptian Government shall, within the limits of its powers resulting from the Firmans, and under the conditions provided for in the present Treaty, take the necessary measures for insuring the execution of the said Treaty.

In case the Egyptian Government shall not have sufficient means at its disposal, it shall call upon the Imperial Ottoman Government, which shall take the necessary measures to respond to such appeal; shall give notice thereof to the Signatory Powers of the Declaration of London of the 17th March, 1885; and shall, if necessary, concert with them on the subject.

The provisions of Articles IV, V, VII, and VIII shall not interfere with the measures which shall be taken in virtue of the present Article.

Article X

Similarly, the provisions of Articles IV, V, VII, VIII, shall not interfere with the measures which His Majesty the Sultan and His Highness the Khedive, in the name of His Imperial Majesty, and within the limits of the Firmans granted, might find it necessary to take for securing by their own forces the defence of Egypt and the maintenance of public order.

In case His Imperial Majesty the Sultan, or His Highness the Khedive, should find it necessarv to avail themselves of the exceptions for which this Article provides, the Signatory Powers of the Declaration of London shall be notified thereof by the Imperial Ottoman Government.

It is likewise understood that the provisions of the four Articles aforesaid shall in no case occasion any obstacle to the measures which the Imperial Ottoman Government may think it necessary to take in order to insure by its own forces the defence of its other possessions situated on the eastern coast of the Red Sea.

Article XI

The measures which shall be taken in the cases provided for by Articles IX and X of the present Treaty shall not interfere with the free use of the Canal. In the same cases, the erection of permanent fortifications contrary to the provisions of Article VIII is prohibited.

Article XII

The High Contracting Parties, by application of the principle of equality as regards the free use of the Canal, a principle which forms one of the bases of the present Treaty, agree that none of them shall endeavour to obtain with respect to the Canal territories or commercial advantages or privileges in any international arrangements which may be concluded. Moreover, the rights of Turkey as the territorial Power are reserved.

Article XIII

With the exception of the obligations expressly provided by the clauses of the present Treaty, the sovereign rights of His Imperial Majesty the Sultan and the rights and immunities of His Highness the Khedive, resulting from the Firmans, are in no way affected.

Article XIV

The High Contracting Parties agree that the engagements resulting from the present Treaty shall not be limited by the duration of the Acts of Concession of the Universal Suez Canal Company.

Article XV

The stipulations of the present Treaty shall not interfere with the sanitary measures in force in Egypt.

Article XVI

The High Contracting Parties undertake to bring the present Treaty to the knowledge of the States which have not signed it, inviting them to accede to it.

Article XVII

The present Treaty shall be ratified, and the ratifications shall be exchanged at Constantinople, within the space of one month, or sooner, if possible.

In faith of which the respective Plenipotentiaries have signed the present Treaty, and have affixed to it the seal of their arms.

Done at Constantinople,
the 29th of the month of October,
in the year 1888.

Note. Great Britain, though she respected this Convention, did not formally adhere to it until the signature of the Anglo-French Agreement of April 8th, 1904, and then on the condition that paragraphs (i) and (ii) of Article VIII should remain in abeyance. After the Great War the "enemy" Powers who had signed the Convention agreed to the replacing of Turkey by Great Britain in the Treaty. By Article 152 of the Versailles Treaty "Germany consents in so far as she is concerned, to the transfer to His Britannic Majesty's Government of the powers conferred on His Imperial Majesty the Sultan by the Convention . . ." Declarations to the same effect were signed by Austria (Article 107, Treaty of St. Germain), by Hungary (Article 91, Treaty of Trianon) and by Turkey (Article 109, Treaty of Sèvres and Article 99, Treaty of Lausanne).

APPENDIX THREE

TEXT OF SUDAN AGREEMENT

The Egyptian Government and the Government of the United Kingdom of Great Britain and Northern Ireland (hereinafter called the "United Kingdom Government"), firmly believing in the right of the Sudanese people to Self-Determination and the effective exercise thereof at the proper time and with the necessary safeguard. Have agreed as follows:

Article 1

In order to enable the Sudanese people to exercise Self-Determination in a free and neutral atmosphere, a transitional period providing full Self-Government for the Sudanese shall begin on the day specified in Article 9 below.

Article 2

The transitional period, being a preparation for the effective termination of the dual Administration shall be considered as a liquidation of that Administration. During the transitional period the sovereignty of the Sudan shall be kept in reserve for the Sudanese until Self-Determination is achieved.

Article 3

The Governor-General shall, during the transitional period, be the supreme constitutional authority within the Sudan. He shall exercise his powers as set out in the Self-Government Statute with the aid of a five-member Commission, to be called the Governor-General's Commission, whose powers are laid down in the terms of reference in Annex I to the present Agreement.

Article 4

This Commission shall consist of two Sudanese proposed by the two contracting Governments in agreement, one Egyptian citizen, one citizen of the United Kingdom and one Pakistani citizen, each to be proposed by his respective Government. The appointment of the two Sudanese members shall be subject to the subsequent approval of the Sudanese Parliament when it is elected, and the Parliament shall be entitled to nominate alternative candidates in case of disapproval. The Commission hereby set up will be formally appointed by Egyptian Government decree.

Article 5

The two Contracting Governments agree that, it being a fundamental principle of their common policy to maintain the unity of the Sudan as a single territory, the special powers which are vested in the Governor-General by Article 100 of the Self-Government Statute shall not be exercised in any manner which is in conflict with that policy.

Article 6

The Governor-General shall remain directly responsible to the two Contracting Governments as regards:

(a) External affairs;

(b) Any change requested by the Sudanese Parliament under Article 101 (1) of the Statute for Self-Government as regards any part of that Statute;

(c) Any resolution passed by the Commission which he regards as inconsistent with his responsibilities. In this case he will inform the two Contracting Governments, each of which must give an answer within one month of the date of formal notice. The Commission's resolution shall stand unless the two Governments agree to the contrary.

Article 7

There shall be constituted a Mixed Electoral Commission of seven members. These shall be three Sudanese appointed by the Governor-General with the approval of his Commission, one Egyptian citizen, one citizen of the United States of America, and one Indian citizen. The non-Sudanese members shall be nominated by their respective Governments. The Indian member shall be Chairman of the Commission. The Commission shall be appointed by the Governor-General on the instructions of the two Contracting Governments. The terms of reference of this Commission are contained in Annex II to this Agreement.

Article 8

To provide the free and neutral atmosphere requisite for Self-Determination there shall be established a Sudanization Committee consisting of:

(a) An Egyptian citizen and a citizen of the United Kingdom to be nominated by their respective Governments and subsequently appointed by the Governor-General, together with three Sudanese members to be selected from a list of five names submitted to him by the Prime Minister of the Sudan. The selection and appointment of these Sudanese members shall have the prior approval of the Governor-General's Commission.

(b) One or more members of the Sudan Public Service Commission who will act in a purely advisory capacity without the right to vote.

The function and terms of reference of this Committee are contained in Annex III to this Agreement.

ARTICLE 9

The transitional period shall begin on the day designated as "the appointed day" in Article 2 of the Self-Government Statute. Subject to the completion of Sudanization as outlined in Annex III to this Agreement, the two Contracting Governments undertake to bring the transitional period to an end as soon as possible. In any case this period shall not exceed three years. It shall be brought to an end in the following manner. The Sudanese Parliament shall pass a resolution expressing their desire that arrangements for Self-Determination shall be put in motion and the Governor-General shall notify the two Contracting Governments of this resolution.

ARTICLE 10

When the two Contracting Governments have been formally notified of this resolution the Sudanese Government, then existing, shall draw up a draft law for the election of the Constituent Assembly which it shall submit to Parliament for approval. The Governor-General shall give his consent to the law with the agreement of his Commission. Detailed preparations for the process of Self-Determination, including safeguards assuring the impartiality of the elections and any other arrangements designed to secure a free and neutral atmosphere shall be subject to international supervision. The two Contracting Governments will accept the recommendations of any international body which may be set up to this end.

ARTICLE 11

Egyptian and British Military Forces shall withdraw from the Sudan immediately upon the Sudanese Parliament adopting a resolution expressing its desire that arrangements for Self-Determination be put in motion. The two Contracting Governments undertake to complete the withdrawal of their forces from the Sudan within a period not exceeding three months.

Article 12

The Constituent Assembly shall have two duties to discharge. The first will be to decide the future of the Sudan as one integral whole. The second will be to draw up a constitution for the Sudan compatible with the decision which shall have been taken in this respect, as well as an electoral law for a permanent Sudanese Parliament. The future of the Sudan shall be decided either:

(a) By the Constituent Assembly choosing to link the Sudan with Egypt in any form, or

(b) By the Constituent Assembly choosing complete independence.

Article 13

The two Contracting Governments undertake to respect the decision of the Constituent Assembly concerning the future status of the Sudan and each Government will take all the measures which may be necessary to give effect to its decision.

Article 14

The two Contracting Governments agree that the Self-Government Statute shall be amended in accordance with Annex IV to this Agreement.

Article 15

This Agreement together with its attachments shall come into force upon signature.

Note. By virtue of this Agreement the Sudan elected to become an independent Republic.

APPENDIX FOUR

AN ACCOUNT OF THE NEW EGYPTIAN CONSTITUTION

General Tendencies:

The new Constitution has been derived from the actualities of the life and circumstances of the Egyptian people. It does not emulate foreign constitutions as was the case with that of 1923, which was derived from the Belgian Constitution. The Constitution is of a socialistic nature in which every Egyptian characteristic is clearly manifested. It introduces new constitutional principles, the most important of which are social solidarity and social and economic justice.

The Constitution not only defined the freedoms and rights of Egyptians, but also their duties. It considers a national duty their participation in public life and has shown the means of this participation, either, by addressing the authorities, or, by expressing opinion through plebiscite on matters of importance which concern the vital interests of the country; and also by collaborating with the National Union to achieve the goals of the Revolution and to reconstruct the political, social and economic life of the Nation.

The new Constitution is democratic in the true sense of the term. It did not confine itself to the meaning of the term as is generally used in Constitutional régimes, but achieved a form of direct and practical democracy without losing its essence, which is the actual participation of the citizens in running the affairs of their country.

The Constitution has basically accepted the Presidential system and has invested the legislative powers in one Assembly, the Nation's Assembly.

Covenants of the Constitution:

The Constitution may be divided into six parts.

(1) The first part concerns the Egyptian State. It stipulates that Egypt is an Arab country and that the Egyptians are of the Arab Nation. This is to affirm the strength and unity of the Arabs as a power worth considering in the international sphere. This is a reflection of the strong bonds which exist between Egypt and the Arab States.

The Régime of the State is Republican and Democratic. This is the Régime accepted and upheld by the people.

Its sovereignity is the Nation's and it is invested in her.

The religion of the State is Islam and Arabic the official language.

(2) The second part concerns the fundamental issues of Egyptian society. Here, the principal functions of the State are defined to direct and guide the various authorities of the State. On these foundations, on which Egyptian society is built, social solidarity, social justic, public freedom and security, equality of opportunity for all Egyptians are guaranteed. It stipulates the setting up of the national economy on a sound basis to ensure harmony between the general economic activities and the private ones and to preserve the sanctity of private property, although the Constitution has put a maximum limit to land ownership.

The Constitution stipulates the encouragement of co-operation and the support of co-operative institutions to ensure the fundamental principle of social solidarity. It also defines the role of the State in raising the standard of living by providing all citizens with an adequate standard of living, guards the family system, motherhood and childhood. It also protects the young from exploitation and neglect, and provides assistance to the old, the sick and disabled and provides medical care by establishing sanatoria and hospitals. It stresses the role of the woman in society and in the family and assures the reconciliation between her duties in these two fields. It also states that public service is an obligation and that he who holds it should seek to serve the public as one of the goals of the Revolution. The abolition of social distinctions, the creation of civil titles has been prohibited.

(3) The third part concerns the general rights and duties.

The Egyptian cannot be deprived of his Egyptian nationality, neither can he change it. It cannot be withdrawn from those who acquired it.

Egyptians are equal before the law. They are equal in their rights and their public duties regardless of their race, origin, language or faith.

Liberties of the Individual regarding His Person

Life residence, abode, faith, and religious practices are guaranteed. The Constitution guarantees the freedoms of opinion, scientific research and the person's right in expressing his free opinion and publishing it in every way. It also stresses the freedom of the press, publication and distribution in accordance with the legitimate rights of the people as a whole.

The Constitution also stipulates in this part the general public rights, as the right of education, the right of congregation, the right of creating societies and unions, the right to work which the State endeavours to provide, and the right to be fairly treated in their work.

The Constitution prohibits the wholesale confiscation of property. Specific confiscation is subject to a court sentence.

The Constitution specifies the political rights, the most important of which is the right to vote, which was made not only a right but also an obligation.

As for the compatriots' duties, the Constitution defines them as being the duty to defend the country, the military service, the payment of taxes and respect of public order and the moral code.

(4) The fourth part deals with the authorities in the State.

The Legislative Authority

Legislative authority is vested in one body, the Nation's Assembly. The Assembly has the usual powers of legislation and the supervision over the executive authority.

The rules regulating the methods of electing the members of the Assembly were left to be stated by a special law to be issued at a later date, to ascertain a measure of elasticity and adaptability.

The term of the Assembly is five years.

The Constitution stipulates the right of members to question and interpellate the Ministers. Also their right to submit any general subject to discussion to gain a clarification of the Government's policy on that matter and their right to express their wishes and suggestions to the Government on any public affair.

The Constitution prohibits the members' cumulation of the membership of the Assembly and a public office or the membership of a board of directors of a company for the duration of their membership. Members of the Assembly cannot receive orders and decorations of the State.

Since some of the State matters do not necessitate the promulgation of a special law as they, by nature, lie wholly within the executive domain, such as the budget and the transfer of an appropriation from one section to the other in the budget, the Constitution stipulates that such matters are to be only approved by the Assembly.

The Constitution guarantees for the Assemby members every possible immunity to enable them to carry on their duties. They are immune from arrest or the starting of penal procedures against them without the Assembly's permission, except in the case of *flagrante delicto*. They are also immune from being censured for opinions or ideas uttered in due course of their works in the Assembly or one of its Committees.

Members may not lose their membership unless a majority of two-thirds ordains it.

Limitations were set on the right of the President to dissolve the Assembly. The Assembly cannot be dissolved twice for the same reason, and the Presidential resolution for dissolution should contain the call for new elections.

The Executive Authority

The Constitution adopts the Presidential system. It stipulates that the President is the Head of State and the Chief Executive. The President must be an Egyptian of Egyptian parents, enjoying his civil and political rights, not less than thirty-five years of age, and not related to the ex-royal family that reigned in Egypt.

The procedures to elect the President are as follows:

The Nation's Assembly nominates a candidate for public referendum. The Constitution is thus, on this point, combined between the Parliamentary and the Presidential systems, avoiding at the same time the defects of both. The Presidential term is six years. If the Presidency becomes vacant through decease or resignation, the Chairman of the Assembly takes over the functions of the President for a period not exceeding sixty days until the new President is elected.

As an inevitable result of the Presidential system, it is stipulated that the President forms, in collaboration with the Ministers, the general policy of the Government. The Head of the State is given the functions accorded him in the various Constitutions such as the right of proposing laws and the power of veto, as well as promulgating the two.

He has also the right to pass emergency measures during periods of its dissolution, provided that those resolutions be submitted to the Assembly within fifteen days of the date of their issue if the Assembly was standing, or, at its first meeting, had it been dissolved at the time of their issue. The President is also empowered to pass emergency resolutions which have the power of law in cases of emergencies and by the Assembly's delegation, provided, that the Assembly's delegation to the President in this concern specifies the subject of the emergency resolutions and the duration of this delegated power.

It is plain that the President of the Republic would be the Commander-in-Chief of the Armed Forces and that he would be the authority to declare war with the approval of the Nation's Assembly; and the authority to conclude treaties and to communicate them to the Assembly for ratification; and the authority to declare the state of emergency under the condition of submitting the case to the Assembly within fifteen days with a view to adopting its decision upon it.

He would be the authority to nominate officials and to discharge them and he has the right to pardon or commute penalties.

Among the most important matters included in the draft is the investment in the President of the Republic of the power, after consulting the Nation's Assembly, to refer through plebiscite to the people the vital problems bearing on the country's higher interests. The Constitution, thus, realizes democracy in its most definite form, by increasing the participation of the people in government in a practical, direct and continued way avoiding, in the meantime, the more serious drawbacks generally attached to parliamentary systems which do not bring the people into participation in Government, except on widely separate occasions.

The President is assisted by Ministers whom he appoints and discharges. These services are terminated at the end of his term. Each Minister controls his Ministry and runs it along the lines of the general policy of the Government. It is also possible to appoint Deputy Ministers who are subject to the stipulations regarding the Ministers.

The Constitution has also realized a definite form of co-operation between the legislative and executive authorities through the warrant to Ministers and Deputy Ministers to be Members of the Nation's Assembly. It also allows the appointment among members of the Assemby of Under-Secretaries of State for the affairs of the Nation's Assembly.

The Constitution also laid the foundation of local Governments in Egypt through the stipulation that the Egyptian Republic is divided into administrative units, each of which is qualified to realize its duristic personality; each of those units owning duristic personalities is represented in a Council whose Members are elected by suffrage. The adhesion to those Councils of nominated Members is allowed with a view to ensure the representation of all therein. These representative Councils in the administrative unities will be concerned with all their respective interests and will be authorized to establish and manage public utilities, economic, social, cultural and health services within their boundaries. The State provides these units with their requirements in the technical, administrative and financial spheres.

The Constitution emphazised the importance of National Defence by stipulating the formation of a Higher Council of National Defence under the Chairmanship of the President of the Republic, which handles matters pertaining to the country's security. It has clearly stated that the armed forces belong to the people and that their duty is to defend the country's sovereignty and the security and peace of its territories.

The State alone will constitute those forces. Consequently, no group or organization will be authorized to form any military or quasi-military troops. The State alone will ensure the military training of the youth and the organization of the National Guard.

The Juridical Authority

The Constitution stresses the independence of the Juridical Authority and its officers. Judges are not liable to dismissal. They are independent and are under no authority in their functions besides that of the law. Interference with lawsuits or the affairs of justice is prohibited to any authority. Court sessions will be public unless the court decides to hold it in camera owing to reasons relating to public order or morality. Sentences are issued and enforced in the name of the Nation.

Law prescribes the terms and conditions for the nomination of members of Parquet and their dismissal. It will regulate the functions of the General Parquet, its competence and its relation to the Juridical Corps.

Law will regulate the Constitution of Military Courts; their competence and the requirements to be met by those who act as judges in same.

(5) The fifth part includes general provisions regarding the capital of the Republic, the national flag and its emblem.

It also includes the stipulation that laws will be only effective in cases posterior to their promulgation.

It also includes the dates of the publication of laws in the official journal and the dates of their effectiveness.

This part also defines the procedure for the amendment of the Constitution and referring the matter finally to the will of the people through plebiscite.

The Constitution, in order to ensure and guarantee the Constitution of laws, decrees, orders, regulations and decisions issued prior to itself stipulates the continuance of their effectiveness and excludes the possibility of their cancellation or modification except under the general rules stipulated by the Constitution.

(6) The sixth part includes transitory rules assumed by the act of transition from the present system to the new system. Most important among these is the congregation of the citizens in a National Union to endeavour for the achievement of the objectives sought by the Revolution and to erect a sound structure of the Nation in the political, social and economic spheres.

June 23rd 1956 has been fixed for a Universal Plebiscite on two counts. (1) The election of the President of the Republic. (2) Vote for or against this Constitution which will start its validity as from the date of the announcement of its approval by the people in the plebiscite. Until that date the Constitutional announcement of February 10, 1953, will remain in force.

APPENDIX FIVE

KEY ARTICLES IN THE COVENANT OF THE LEAGUE OF THE ARAB STATES

Signed 22nd March, 1945

Article II

The object of the League shall be to strengthen the ties between the participant States, to co-ordinate their political programmes in such a way as to effect real collaboration between them, to preserve their independence and sovereignty, and to consider in general the affairs and interests of the Arab countries.

Likewise, a further object shall be the close collaboration of the participant States, in accordance with the régime and conditions prevailing in each (individual) State, in the following matters:

(1) Economic and financial affairs,
(2) Communications,
(3) Cultural affairs,
(4) Matters relating to nationality,
(5) Matters relating to social questions,
(6) Matters relating to public health.

Article VIII

Each State participant in the League shall respect the existing régime obtaining in the other League States, regarding it as a (fundamental) right of those States, and pledges itself not to undertake any action tending to alter that régime.

Article XIX

Those Arab States desirous of closer collaboration with each other, and stronger ties than those specified by this Covenant, have a right to conclude such agreements between themselves towards the realization of these objects, as they desire.

Treaties and Agreements previously concluded, or which may be concluded with any other State, by any State belonging to the League, shall not be obligatory or binding on the other members.

Article XVII

The States participant in the League shall deposit with the Secretariat General texts of all the Treaties and Agreements which they have concluded or may conclude with any other State belonging to, or outside the League.

Article XIX

Amendments to the Covenant by a two-thirds majority.

Article V

Deals with disputes between member States.

Article VI

Deals with aggression against members.

Appendices

(a) Special appendix relating to Palestine.

(b) Special appendix relating to co-operation with the Arab countries non-participant in the League Council.

MACHINERY OF THE LEAGUE

The Council of the League

Composed of representatives of member States, each having a single vote.

Functions (Art. III)

(a) Realization of the objects mentioned in Art. II; (b) to give effect to agreements concluded between members; (c) to decide upon methods of collaboration with international organizations.

Decisions (Art. VII)

(a) Obligatory on all if unanimous; (b) if by majority vote, shall be obligatory on those who accept them.

Meetings (Art. XI)

(a) Twicc a year each March and October; (b) extraordinary sessions on the request of two members.

Secretariat (Art. XII)

(a) Permanent secretariat general; (b) Secretary General appointed by two-thirds majority; (c) in consultation with the Council, he appoints Assistant Secretaries and principal officials.

Committees (Art. IV)

For each subject specified in Art, II a special Committee shall be formed. Existing Committees (Political, Economic, Social and Cultural, Financial and Administrative, Legal).

Functions

Formulating the bases, extent, and form of collaboration, in the shape of draft-agreements to the Council.

TRIPARTITE DECLARATION (U.K., U.S.A., FRANCE)

Declared:

(1, 2) The three Western Powers, confirm their opposition to the development of an arms race between the Arab States and Israel; and that all applications for arms or war material from these countries would be considered in the light of their self-defence and their part in the defence of the area as a whole.

(3) Their desire to promote peace and stability in the area; and their opposition to the use of force or threat of force between the States in that area. They would take action, consistently with obligations as members of the United Nations, to prevent violations of frontiers or armistice lines.

THE INTER-ARAB JOINT DEFENCE ALLIANCE AND ECONOMIC PACT

(a) Adopted by a majority of the Council of the League on 13th April, 1950.

(b) Came into force, having been ratified by Egypt, Syria, (1951), Jordan, Iraq and Saudi Arabia (1952).

Key Articles

Article II

The signatories consider aggression against any one of them as aggression against all and to undertake to help victims of such an aggression (according to Art. IV of the Covenant and Art. 51 of the Charter).

Article III

At the invitation of any one signatory all were to consult together whenever there were reasonable grounds for believing that the territorial integrity, independence or security of any one were threatened. In the event of a risk of war all would immediately "unify their military plans and defensive measures as the situation may demand".

Article IV

All signatories are to co-operate in the development and co-ordination of their armed forces and to participate, according to their resources and needs, in preparing, individually and collectively, the means to resist aggression.

Article V

The establishment of a Permanent Military Commission composed of representatives of the General Staff of their forces (headquarters in Cairo).

Article VI

The establishment of a Joint Defence Council consisting of Ministers of Foreign Affairs and Defence assisted by the Permanent Military Commission, under the control of the Council of the League, for the implementation of Articles II, III, IV and V. Decisions of this Council, binds all members by a two-thirds majority.

Articles VII, VIII

The establishment of an Economic Council consisting of Ministers in charge of economic developments, etc.

Article XII

Duration of Pact, ten years from date of ratification.

Article XIII

The Pact comes into force fifteen days after ratification by at least four States.

Note. A Military supplement exists for organizing the machinery of the Pact, and the functions of the permanent Military Commission.

APPENDIX SIX

THE NASSER TESTAMENT

NOTE. It is often unwise and misleading to judge a revolution by foreign standards. In the case of Egypt it is, also, largely unnecessary. For Colonel Nasser has written his Testament, to my mind one of the most revealing documents of modern history. It is repetitive and, sometimes, redundant, but it is the story of the revolution developing in the mind and heart of a man.

It is quoted in full, below.

"It is not true that the Revolution of July 23rd started on account of the results of the war in Palestine. Nor was it caused by defective arms, to which officers and men fell victims. It is still further from the truth to attribute it to the crisis of the elections of the Officers' Club. In my opinion its causes are deeper and farther. Had the officers endeavoured to avenge themselves because they cheated in Palestine or because the defective arms strained their nerves and because they suffered an indignity in the elections of the Officers' Club, the whole affair would not have deserved to be called a revolution. A mere mutiny was the likely description even if it were attributed to causes fair and just in themselves. All these were incidental. Perhaps their greatest influence was that they urged us to march forward along the road to revolution; but without them we were marching just the same.

"To-day I am trying to recall all the events that passed and, after years have elapsed since we first thought of the reovlution, to go back to the first day I discovered the seeds of revolt within me. That day lies farther in my life than November 1951, which marked the beginning of the crisis of the Officers' Club elections. The organization of the Liberal Officers was then existing and active. I do not exaggerate when I say that the crisis of the Officers' Club elections was caused, more than anything else, by the activities of the Liberal Officers. We were determined to fight then in order to test the strength of our mass formation and real organization.

"That day lies again farther in my life than the beginning of the scandal of defective arms. The Liberal Officers' Organization had existed before. Their circulars gave the first warning of the impending tragedy. Behind the uproar that rose on account of the defective arms their activities lay. Nay, that day goes back still farther in my life than May 16th, 1944, which marked the start of my life in the Palestinian War. As I trace the details of our experience in Palestine I feel a strange sensation. We were fighting in Palestine but our dreams were in Egypt. Our bullets were aimed at the enemy lurking in the trenches in front of us, but our hearts were hovering round our distant Mother Country, which was then a prey to the wolves that ravaged it. In Palestine Liberal Officers' cells were meeting in trenches and posts, studying and searching. And it was in Palestine that Salah Salem and Zakaria Mohyy-el-Din came to me after having penetrated the siege of Falouga; there we sat besieged neither knowing what was to become of that siege nor when would it end. We spoke of nothing but our country and how to deliver it. It was in Palestine that Kamal El Dine Hussein sat beside me one day and spoke as his eyes wandered and his thoughts dispersed; 'Do you know what Ahmed Abdel Aziz had told me before he died?' he asked. 'What did he say?' I asked in return. With a deep tone of voice and still deeper look he said, ''Listen Kamal, Egypt is the field of our supreme war effort.''

"In Palestine I met not only friends that shared the work for Egypt, but there I also discovered the thoughts that shed their light on the road ahead. I remember the days I spent in trenches pondering over our problems. Falouga was then besieged and the enemy had concentrated his guns and aircraft heavily and terribly upon it. Often have I said to myself, 'Here we are in these underground holes besieged. How we were cheated into a war unprepared and how our destinies have been the plaything of passions, plots and greed. Here we lay under fire unarmed.'

"As I reached that stage in my thinking, my feelings would suddenly jump across the battlefront, across frontiers to Egypt. I found myself saying, 'There is our Mother-Country, a far, far bigger Falouga. What is happening in Palestine is but a miniature picture of what was happening in Egypt. Our Mother-Country has been likewise besieged by difficulties as well as ravaged by an enemy. She was cheated and pushed to fight unprepared. Greed, intrigue and passion have toyed with it and left it under fire unarmed.'

"Besides, it was not only the friends I met in Palestine who spoke to me of the future of our country, not only the experience that I had gathered there that hammered at my mind with warnings and forebodings as to its destiny; but the enemy also played his part in reminding us of our homeland and its difficulties. A few months ago I read some articles written upon me by a Jewish officer named Yerdan Cohen. These were published in the *Jewish Observer*. In these articles he related how he met me during the contacts and discussions of the Armistice. 'The subject that Gamal Abdel Nasser discussed with me,' he stated, 'was Israel's struggle against the English, how we organized our underground resistance in Palestine and how we succeeded in mobilizing world public opinion behind us against them.'

"The day I discovered the seeds of revolt within me was still further back than February 4, 1942. I wrote to a friend later saying, 'What is to be done now that the catastrophe has befallen us, and after we have accepted it, surrendered to it and taken it submissively and meekly. I really believe,' I continued, 'that Imperialism is playing a one-card game in order to threaten only. If ever it knew that there were Egyptians ready to shed their blood and to meet force by force it would withdraw and recoil like a harlot. This, of course, is the state or habit of Imperialism everywhere.'[1] That event had a new influence on the spirit and feeling of the army and ourselves. Henceforth officers spoke not of corruption and pleasure, but of sacrifice and of their willingness to give up their lives to save their country's dignity. They all repented they did not intervene, however weak they may have obviously been, to redeem their country's honour and to wash away this shame with their very blood. But let us wait. To-morrow will soon be here.

"Some have tried to revenge this but the time for revenge had gone. Hearts were full of fire and sorrow.

"The fact is that that blow brought life back to some and made them realize that they should be prepared to defend their honour. That, in itself, was a severe lesson.

"That day is again far more distant in my life than the feverish days I lived as a student, marching in demonstrations, clamouring for the restoration of the 1923 Constitution which was duly restored in 1935, and when I used to join delegations of students calling on

[1] During the war, the British surrounded King Farouk and dictated the future personnel and policy of the Egyptian Government which, they imputed, had pro-Nazi sympathies, and was plannng a "stab-in-the-back" to the British forces in North Africa.

leaders in their homes and demanding from them to unite for the sake of Egypt; and as a result of these efforts the National Front was formed in 1936. I remember that during the period of boiling over I wrote on September 2nd, 1935 to a friend of mine, now Dr. Aly El Nashar, the following letter:

"'Brother Aly,

"'On August 30th I telephoned your father enquiring after you. He informed me you were at school. I therefore decided to write what I had intended to convey to you by telephone. The Lord hath said, "Prepare for them (the enemy) whatever force you can", but where is that force we prepare? The present situation is critical and Egypt is in a still more critical position.'

"I wonder when it was that I discovered the seeds of revolt within me. I consider that such seeds were not embedded in my heart alone and that I found them in the very hearts of others who could not themselves trace them to their origin in themselves. It seems clear that these seeds were innate in us; they lay dormant and inherited in our souls, a legacy from a previous generation.

"I have but two things to mention in this connection. First are some feelings taking a vague form of a hope at the beginning and later becoming a definite idea and a practical plan prior to midnight July 23rd. Secondly are some experiences that carried those feelings with their vague hope, their definite idea and practical plan into execution at midnight July 23rd and onwards until now.

"It is these feelings and experiences that I would like to discuss. One question has persistently occurred to me; was it our duty, as an army, to do what we did on July 23rd 1952? I have just explained how the Revolution of July 23rd was the realization of a hope that dangled before the eyes of the people of Egypt since they began, in modern times, to think of governing themselves and having the final word on their destiny.

"If this be so, and if what took place on July 23rd was only a military mutiny and not a popular revolt, why was the army then, apart from any other forces, destined to carry out this Revolution?

"Throughout my life I have had faith in militarism. The soldier's sole duty is to die on the frontiers of his country. Why then was our army compelled to act in the capital and not on the frontier?

"Once more, let me reiterate that the defeat in Palestine, the defective arms, the crisis of the Officers' Club election were not the real springs from which the current flowed. They may have accelerated the flood but they could never be the original source. Why then did this duty fall upon the Army? This question has often occurred to me. It came to me persistently during the stage of hoping, of thinking and of planning before July 23rd. It repeated itself several times during the experimental period after July 23rd. We had different factors to justify action before July 23rd and to explain to us why it was imperative that the Army should act. 'If the Army does not move,' we said to ourselves, 'who else will?' We were the ghost with which the tyrant haunted the dreams of the nation. It was high time that the same ghost turned against the tyrant and upset his dreams. Other things we said; but what was most significant of all is the feeling deep down in our consciousness that this was our duty. If we did not perform it we would betray the sacred trust in our charge. I admit that the complete picture was not yet vivid in my imagination until I went through a long stage of experience after July 23rd. The very details of this experience were in themselves the details of this picture.

"I confess that after July 23rd I suffered fits in which I accused myself, my colleagues and the rest of the Army of rashness and folly we committed on July 23rd.

'Prior to that date I imagined that the whole nation was on tiptoes and prepared for action, that it awaited the advance of the vanguard and the storming of the outside walls for it to pour down in a solid phalanx marching faithfully to the great goal. I thought we were only the pioneers and the commandoes, that we would be soon followed by the solid masses marching to the goal. My imagination often carried me away. I felt I could hear the rattle of their solid, orderly rows as they marched onwards to the main front. My faith was such as to render everything I heard a concrete fact and not a mere vision.

"After July 23rd I was shocked by the reality. The vanguard performed its task; it stormed the walls of the fort of tyranny; it forced Farouk to abdicate and stood by expecting the mass formations to arrive at their ultimate object. It waited and waited. Endless crowds showed up, but how different is the reality from the vision! The multitudes that arrived were dispersed followers and contrasted remnants. The holy march towards the great goal was interrupted. A dismal picture, horrible and threatening, then presented itself. I felt my heart charged with sorrow and dripping with bitterness. The mission of the vanguard had not ended. In fact it was just beginning at that very hour. We needed discipline but found chaos behind our lines. We needed unity but found dissensions. We needed action but found nothing but surrender and idleness. It was from this source and no other that the Revolution derived its motto.

"If I were asked then what I required most my instant answer would be 'To hear but one Egyptian uttering one word of justice about another, to see but one Egyptian not devoting his time to criticize wilfully the ideas of another, to feel that there was but one Egyptian ready to open his heart for forgiveness, indulgence and loving his brother Egyptians.' Personal and persistent selfishness was the rule of the day. The word 'I' was on every tongue. It was the magic solution of every difficulty and the effective cure for every malady. Often did I meet men, referred to in the press as 'great men', of various tendencies and colours, from whom I sought the solution of a difficult problem. I could hear nothing from them save the word 'I'. He and only he was capable of understanding the problems of economics; the rest were but children creeping on all fours. He and only he was the expert statesman and the rest only learning their *a* and *b* and had not got to *c*. After interviewing any of these men I would go back to my colleagues bitterly exclaiming, 'How utterly futile. . . ! If we were to ask that man about a difficulty in fishing off the Islands of Hawaii his answer would only be "I".'

"I remember I once visited one of our universities and sat with professors endeavouring to profit by the experience of men of learning. Many spoke and spoke at length. Unfortunately not one of them presented a new idea. Every one introduced himself and listed his moral capacities which, in his view, could perform miracles. Every one eyed me as if I were to him more precious than the treasures of earth or the blessings of eternity. I could not help but remark to them all 'Everyone in his place can perform miracles. The primary duty is to put all energy into it and if you, as university professors, ever thought of students and rendered them, as you should, your principal care, you would provide us with a tremendous force wherewith to build up our country. Let every one remain at his post and strive hard at it. Do not look up to us. Circumstances have compelled us to leave our posts to perform a sacred task. We sincerely wish the country has no further use for us save as professional soldiers in the Army. There we would have remained.' I did not wish then to set before them the example of the members of the Revolution Council who, before the crisis summoned them for the supreme task, were performing their duties in the Army most diligently. I did not wish tell[1] them that most of the members of the Revolution Council were professors in the Staff College . . . a clear proof of their distinction as professional soldiers. Neither did I wish to mention to them that three members of the Revolution Council had received promotion on the field in Palestine, lest I should be regarded as if I were boasting of my brethren and colleagues of the Revolution Council.

"I admit the situation caused me a depressing psychological crisis. But, later, experience and reflection, and the true significance I derived from them lightened the reaction of the crisis upon me and made me seek pretexts from the world of reality that came to me when the complete picture of the state of my country became clear to me. It, moreover, provided me with the answer to the question which was always in my mind. That question is: 'Was it our duty, the Army's duty, to act as it did on July 23rd?' The unavoidable and unescapable answer is 'Yes'.

"I can now say that we are at present in the throes of two revolutions and not one.

"Every nation on earth undergoes two revolutions: one political, in which it recovers its right for self-government from an imposed despot, or an aggressive Army occupying its territory without its consent. The second revolution is social, in which the classes of society would struggle against each other until justice for all countrymen has been gained and conditions have become stable.

"Other nations have preceded us along the path of human progress and passed through the two revolutions but not simultaneously. Hundreds of years separated the one from the other. In the case of our nation, it is going through the two revolutions together and at the same time,[2] a great experiment putting us to the test. This great experiment is due to the fact that the conditions of each revolution are remarkably different, strangely discordant and terrifically clashing. Political revolution demands, for its success, the unity of all

[1] I have not altered the English of Colonel Nasser's Testament. I think its individuality makes his argument more trenchant. It is, in fact, a translation.

[2] Elsewhere Colonel Nasser has said that, in fact, Egypt is undergoing three revolutions: the political, the economic and the social.

national elements, their fusion and mutual support, as well as self-denial for the sake of the country as a whole.

"One of the first signs of social revolution is that values are shaken and creeds are relaxed; fellow-countrymen struggle against each other, individuals and classes. Corruption, suspicion, hatred and selfishness dominate them. Between the anvil and the hammer we now live in two revolutions: one demanding that we should unite together, love one another and strain every nerve to reach our goal; the other forces us, in spite of ourselves, to disperse and give way to hatred, everyone thinking only of himself.

Between the anvil and the hammer the 1919 Revolution was lost and failed to achieve the results which it ought to have realized. The ranks that massed in 1919 to face tyranny were, after a while, occupied only by internal strife. Tyranny became more arbitrary whether it was in the form of the open forces of occupation or their veiled cat's paws, headed by Sultan Fouad and later by his son Farouk. The nation reaped nothing but a crop of self-suspicion, egoism and hatred, between individuals and classes alike. The hopes which the 1919 Revolution was expected to realize faded. The fact that they faded and that they did not die out is due to that natural resistance which the hopes that our nation always entertained, bring forth. This resistance was still alive then and preparing for another trial. Such was the state of affairs that prevailed after the 1919 Revolution and which compelled the Army to be the only force capable of action.

"The situation demanded that a homogeneous force should emerge away, to a certain extent, from the struggle of individuals and classes. This force should issue from the heart of the people. Its members should have faith in each other and should have in their hands such elements of material force as to ensure swift and decisive action. Such conditions did not prevail except in the Army.

"It was not the Army, as I mentioned, that determined its role in the events. The opposite is nearer the truth. It was the events and their evolution that determined for the Army its role in the mighty struggle for the liberation of the country.

"I have realized from the very beginning that our success depended on our complete understanding of the nature of the conditions we live in as related to our national history. We were not in a position to change these conditions by a mere stroke of the pen. We were not also in a position to put back or put forward the hands of the clock and dominate time. We could not act, along the route of history, as the traffic constable does on the road by stopping the passage of one revolution to let through another, and therefore avoid a collision. The only thing to do was to act as best we could, and escape being crushed between the two mill-stones.

"It was imperative that we should proceed with the two revolutions together. The day we marched along the path of political revolution and dethroned Farouk we took a similar step along the path of social revolution by limiting the ownership of agricultural land. I still believe until to-day that the Revolution of July 23rd should retain its capacity for swift action and initiative in order that it may fulfil the miracle of proceeding with the two revolutions simultaneously, contradictory as our action may appear to be sometimes.

"When a friend of mine came to me one day exclaiming, 'You asked for unity to face the English and at the same time you permit the Graft Court to proceed with its work,' I listened to him with the image of our big crisis in my mind: the crisis of being between the two mill-stones. One revolution demanded that we should stand in one row and forget the past, another revolution forcing us to restore the lost dignity of moral values and not forget the past.

"I did not say to my friend that the only way out to safety was, as I mentioned, the capacity for swift action and initiative as well as the capacity for marching along the two paths together.

"This was not my will; nor was it the will of those who took part in the Revolution of July 23rd. It was the will of fate, of the history of our nation and the stage it is passing through to-day.

"What is it we want to do? And which is the way to it?

"The truth is that I often knew the answer to the first question. Such knowledge was not confined to me; it was the hope that our whole generation has unanimously held.

"As for the answer to the second question; namely the way to that which we want, I confess it has undergone in my mind as many changes as nothing else has done. I almost believe that it is the biggest bone of contention in this generation.

"There is no doubt we all dream of Egypt free and strong. No Egyptian would ever differ with another about that.

"As for the way to liberation and strength, that is the most intricate problem in our lives. I had faced this complex problem prior to July 23rd, 1952. I continued to face it after that, until its many angles, which had lain hidden under the shadows that fell upon them, became clear to me. I began to behold horizons which were shrouded out of my sight by the pall of darkness that fell on our country for centuries.

"I have felt, since consciousness first dawned within me, that positive action is the only way. But what action? The word positive action may appear on paper sufficient to solve the problem. But, in life as well as in the difficult circumstances our generation has been going through, and in this crisis that ravaged deeply by into the destinies of our country, it was not sufficient. At one stage of my life enthusiasm meant positive action as a means of appreciating. Then my ideal in positive action changed until I came to realize that it was not enough that my nerves alone should cry out, and that I must communicate my enthusiasm to others until their nerves also cry out.

"In those days I was at the head of demonstrations in Al Nahda School. From the bottom of my heart I clamoured demanding complete independence; others repeated my cries; but these were in vain.

"They were blown away by the winds and became faint echoes that do not move mountains or smash rocks. Later 'positive action' meant in my opinion that all leaders of Egypt should unite on one thing. Our rebellious cheering crowds passed their homes one by one demanding, in the name of the youth of Egypt, that they should unite on one thing. It was a tragedy to my faith that the one thing they united on was the Treaty of 1936.[1]

"Then came the Second World War and the events that preceded it. Both inflamed our youth and spread fire to its innermost feelings. We, the whole generation, began to move towards violence. I confess, and I hope the Attorney-General will not incriminate me on account of this confession, that political assassinations blazed in my inflamed mind during that period as the only positive action from which we could not escape, if we were to save the future of our country.

"I thought of assassinating many whom I regarded as obstacles between our country and its future. I began to expose their crimes and set myself as a judge of their actions and of the harm that these

[1] The Anglo-Egyptian Treaty that governed relations between Britain and Egypt until 1953.

brought upon the country; and then I would follow all this by the sentence that should be passed upon them.

"I thought of assassinating the ex-King and those of his men who tampered with our sacred traditions. In this I was not alone. When I sat with others our thoughts passed from thinking to planning. Many a design did I draw up those days. Many a night did I lie awake preparing the means for the expected positive action. Our life was, during this period, like an exciting detective story. We had great secrets; we had symbols; we hid in the darkness and arranged our pistols and bombs side by side. Those were the hope we dreamt of. We made many attempts in this direction and I still remember, until to-day, our feelings and emotions as we dashed along the road to its end.

"The truth, however, is I did not feel at ease within myself to consider violence as the positive action essential for the salvation of our country's future. I had within me a feeling of distraction which was a mixture of complex and intermingled factors: of patriotism, religion, compassion, cruelty, faith, suspicion, knowledge and ignorance.

"Slowly and gently did the idea of political assassination, which was blazing in my imagination, begin to die out and lose its value within me as the realization of the expected positive action.

"I remember one night in particular which was decisive in directing my thoughts and my dreams along that channel. We had prepared everything necessary for action. We selected one, whom we found essential to put out of the way. We studied the circumstances of the life of this individual, and made the plot in detail. This plot was to shoot him as he returned home at night. We organized a squad of assault which would shoot him, another to guard this first and a third to organize the plan of getting away to safety after the plot had been fully carried out.

"The appointed night came and I went out myself with the squad of execution. Everything went to plan as we imagined.

"The scene was empty, as we had expected. The squads lay in the hiding places fixed for them. The person whom we wanted to get out of the way came and bullets were fired at him. The squad of execution withdrew, covered in its retreat by the guards, and the operation of getting away began. I started my motor car and dashed away from the scene of the positive action we planned. Cries. wailings and moans suddenly rang in my ears. The wailing of a woman, the voice of a scared child and the continuous feverish appeals for help assailed my ears. I was steeped in my rebellious set of emotions as my car rushed me along. I then became conscious of something strange; the sounds I heard were still tearing my ears, as well as the cries, wails and moans and the feverish appeals for help. I was then away from the scene, further than sound could reach. Nevertheless, I felt all these beginning to haunt and chase me.

"I got home, threw myself on my bed, my mind in a fever, my heart and conscience incessantly boiling. The cries, moans and wails and the appeals for help still rang in my ears. All night long I could not sleep. I lay on my bed in darkness, lighting one cigarette after another, wandering away with my rebellious thoughts, which were driven away by the sounds that haunted me. 'Was I right?' I asked myself. With conviction I answered: 'My motives were patriotic.' 'Was this an unavoidable means?' I again asked myself. In doubt I replied: 'What could we have done otherwise? Is it possible that the future of our country could change by getting rid of this one individual or another? Is not the question far deeper than this?' In bewilderment I would say to myself: 'I almost feel that the question is deeper. We dream of the glory of a nation. Which is more important? That some one should pass away who should pass away or that someone should come who should come?'

"As I mention this I see rays of light gradually filtering through these crowded sensations. 'What is important,' I would say to myself, 'is that someone should come who should come. We are dreaming of the glory of a nation: a glory that must be built up.' As I tossed on my bed in a room full of smoke and charged with emotions, I found myself asking: 'And then?' 'And what then?' a mysterious voice called out. With deep conviction this time I again said to myself, 'Our method must change. This is not the positive action we should aim at. The roots of the question go more deeply. The problem is more serious and more far-reaching.' At this I felt an undiluted relief which was soon dispersed by the cries, moans and wails and appeals whose echoes resounded inside me. Suddenly I found myself exclaiming, 'I wish he would not die.' It was indeed strange that dawn would find me wishing life for someone I wished he was dead the night before. I rushed anxiously to the morning papers. I was happy to find that the individual whose assassination I plotted was destined to live.

"But this was not the fundamental problem. The principal question is to find out the positive action. Since then we began to think of something more deeply rooted, more serious and more far-reaching. We began to draw the preliminary lines of the vision that was realized in the night of July 23rd, namely, a revolution springing from the very heart of the people, charged with its aspirations and pursuing completely the steps it had previously taken along its destined path.

"I began this discourse with two questions: one was this: 'What is it we want to do?' and the second: 'Which is the way to what we want to do?' The answer of the first question, as I mentioned, was a hope unanimously held. The answer of the second question, about the way to do what we want, I discussed at length until July 23rd.

"But was what happened on July 23rd all that we wanted to do? The answer is emphatically 'No', since that was only the first step along the road.

"The ecstasy of success on July 23rd did not really deceive me. It did not appear to me as if it had realized our hopes or that spring had come. The opposite may be the truth. Every moment carried to me a fresh success of the Revolution, but it also laid unwittingly a heavy burden upon my shoulders. I mentioned that before July 23rd I thought the whole nation was standing on tip-toes and ready for action and that it had awaited but the storming of the walls by the vanguard for it to rush forward behind the vanguard in mass formations marching orderly onwards. I stated that our role as a vanguard could not take but a few minutes to perform, after which we would be followed by the massed regular forces. I also drew up in that part of the picture the disputes, chaos, hatred and passions which were let loose, each trying by its egoism to exploit the Revolution for its purposes. I said and I shall go on saying that this was the most cruel shock I ever felt in my life. But I admit I should have expected all that happened since it was impossible to fulfil our dreams by merely pressing an electric button, and since it was impossible that the scum and débris of centuries could disappear in the twinkle of an eye.

"It was easy then, and I still find it easy now, to shed the blood of ten, twenty, or thirty persons in order to strike fear and panic in the hearts of many hesitants, and thus force them to swallow their passions, their hatred and their whims.[1] But what result could such an action achieve? I used to think that the only way to face a problem was to trace it to its origin and to try to follow the source from which it began. It was not just to impose 'The Reign of Blood' upon us, regardless of the historical circumstances which our nation has been through and which left its imprint upon us and made us what we are to-day. I said once that I did not pretend to be a professor of history; for this is the last thing my imagination would aspire to. I said that I would make my attempts only as a child beginning its history course at school.

"Fate has so willed that we should be on the crossroads of the world. Often have we been the road which invaders took and a prey to adventurers. In certain circumstances we found it impossible to explain the factors latent in the soul of our nation without due consideration of these circumstances.

"In my opinion we cannot overlook the history of Egypt under the Pharaohs or the reaction between the Greek spirit and ours, the Roman invasion, and Muslim conquest and the waves of Arab migrations that followed.

"I believe we should pause for a time and examine the circumstances we went through in the Middle Ages; for it is these that got us up to the stage we are in to-day.

"If the crusades were the dawn of a renaissance in Europe they were also the commencement of the dark ages in our country. Our nation has borne the brunt of the crusades. They left it exhausted, poverty-stricken and destitute. At the same time that it was menaced by the war, it suffered tyranny and lay prostrate under the spikes of the horses of the despots of Inner Asia. These were slaves when they first came. Then they turned against their masters and replaced them as princes. They were brought to Egypt in droves as Mameluke slaves and after spending a time in this good and peaceful country they became kings. Tyranny, oppression and destruction became the characteristic feature of their rule which enveloped Egypt in its blackness for centuries. During that period our country became a forest ruled by wild beasts. The Mamelukes looked upon it as an easy prey. Their struggles turned on the partitioning of the booty. Our souls, our wealth and our land were the spoil.

[1] Colonel Nasser has said he is a sentimentalist, not a dictator, but the language he uses here is curiously personal.

"Often, when I go back to turning the pages of our history, I feel sorrow tearing my soul as I consider the period when a tyrannical feudalism was formed, a feudalism which had no other object save sucking the blood of life out of our veins and sapping from these veins the remnants of any feeling of power and of dignity. It left in the depth of our souls an effect that we have to struggle to overcome.

"In point of fact, when I visualize this effect, I feel I can understand, on most occasions, some of the symptoms of our political life.

"It often appears to me that many adopt, towards the Revolution, an attitude of spectators who have no other interest except waiting to see the result of the battle in which two sides, with whom they have not the least connection, are struggling. I often rebel against this attitude and say to myself and to some of my friends: 'Why don't they come forward? Why don't they emerge from the hiding-places, wherein they put themselves, to speak and move?'

"I do not find an explanation for this save the deposits of the Mameluke reign, when princes used to wrestle against each other, and when horsemen fought in the streets, while people rushed to their homes, locking themselves therein, in order to be away from the fight which did not concern them.

"It often appears to me that we resort to our imagination and demand that it should fulfil our desires in the sphere of fancy; we enjoy this fancy and thus rest too inactive to try to realize it.

"Many of us have not yet rid ourselves of this feeling; many have not assimilated the idea that this country is theirs and that they are its masters and the leaders of opinion and the proper authorities therein.

"I have endeavoured once to understand an expression I used often to shout as a child when I saw planes flying in the sky. I used to say:

"'Oh, God Almighty! Would that a calamity betake the English!' I found out later that we inherited the expression from our forefathers in the days of the Mamelukes. It was not then applied to the English, but it was modified by us or by the unchanged and latent deposits in us. We only changed the name of the oppressor. Our forefathers used to say: 'Oh, God Almighty! Send the Osmanly to perdition!'

"In the same unchanged spirit the idea was often expressed by our tongues. The name English replaced the name Osmanli, in accordance with the political changes that subsequently followed upon Egypt between the two epochs.

"Then what happened after the Mameluke period? The French expedition came. The iron curtain that the Tartars imposed on us was torn away. New ideas poured upon us. New horizons, hitherto unknown to us, opened.

"The Dynasty of Mohamed Aly inherited all the conditions of Mameluke life, even though it endeavoured to dress them in the fashionable clothes of the nineteenth century. Our contacts with Europe and the world were resumed anew. Consciousness, in a modern sense, dawned upon us and brought with it a new crisis.

"There is no doubt that this state of affairs was responsible for the absence of a united public opinion in our country. The gulf between one individual and another, and one generation and another, became particularly wide.

"At one time I complained that people did not know what they wanted. They were not unanimous in their choice of the way to take. I realized later that I demanded the impossible and that I took no account of the circumstances of our society.

"We live in a society that has not yet crystallized. It is still boiling over and restless. It has not yet calmed or settled down, so as to continue its gradual evolution parallel with other nations which preceded it along the road.

"I believe, without paying any compliment to people's emotions, that our nation has realized a miracle. Any nation, exposed to the same conditions as our country, could be easily lost. It could be swept away by the torrents that fell upon it. But it stood firm in the violent earthquake.

"It is true we nearly lost our equilibrium in some circumstances; but generally we did not fall to the ground. As I consider one normal Egyptian family out of the thousands that live in the capital, I find the following: the father, for example, is a turbanned 'fellah' from the heart of the country; the mother a lady descended from Turkish stock; the sons of the family are at a school adopting the English system; the daughters the French. All this lies between the thirteenth century and the outward appearances of the twentieth.

"Therefore, one may ask: 'Which is the way, and what is our role in it?' The way is that which leads to economic and political freedom.

"Our role is the role of the watchmen only, no more and no less, watchmen for a definite period with a time limit.

"How similar is our nation to-day to a caravan, that had to take a certain route! The route was long; thieves and highwaymen attacked it; it was led astray by the mirage; and finally the caravan dispersed, each group wandering to a different place and every individual taking a different direction.

"How similar is our mission in these circumstances to the part of someone going out of his way to gather these wandering, lost wayfarers in order to put them again on the right track and leave them to proceed with their march!

"This is our part and I cannot imagine any other. If it occurred to me to solve all the problems of our country, I should be a dreamer; and I am not fond of clinging to dreams.

"We have neither the capacity to do this nor the experience to achieve it. Our job is, as I said, to define the landmarks of the road, to lead the wanderers back to where they would resume their march, and to catch up with those who were pursuing the mirage and convince them of the futility of chasing the mirage as they do.

"I fully knew, from the beginning, that our mission would not be an easy one and that it would cost us much of our popularity. We have to speak frankly and speak straight to the minds of the people. Our predecessors used to offer people nothing but dreams, and utter nothing but what people liked to hear.

"How easy it is to speak to people's instincts and how difficult to address their minds! Our instincts are the same, but our minds are subject to diversity and disparity. Egyptian politicians, in the past, were so intelligent as to realize this fact. They aimed their words at the instincts of the people, leaving their minds wandering in the desert. We could do the same. We could charge people's nerves with big words, which are drawn from the world of imagination and which make them perform chaotic actions, for which they did not prepare or make any previous plan. We could leave them to cry their voices hoarse by cheering: 'O, God Almighty, would that a calamity betake the English!', as our forefathers had done under the Mamelukes when they cried, 'Oh, Lord Almighty: send the Osmanly to perdition.'

"Nothing followed their cries. Was this then the mission for which we were destined, and what could we have achieved if we had really gone along that road?

"I have mentioned that the success of the Revolution depends on its comprehension of the real conditions facing it and its capacity for prompt action. To this I now add that it should be free from the effects of glittering words. It should proceed with what it deems its duty, regardless of the price it may pay out of its popularity or of the cheers and the applause it may receive. Otherwise we shall betray the trust we hold for the Revolution and its duties.

"Many people come to me and exclaim, 'You have angered everybody.' To which exclamation I always reply, 'It is not the people's anger that influences the situation. The question should be: "Was what aroused their anger for the good of the country or for the interest of whom?" I realize we have upset big landowners; but was it possible not to upset them and yet behold some of us owning thousands of acres, while others do not own the plot of land wherein they are buried after their death?

"I realize we have aroused the wrath of old politicians; but was it possible not to do so and yet behold our country a victim to their passions, their corruption and their struggle for the spoils of office?

"I realize we have angered many government officials; but without this was it possible to spend more than half the budget on officials' salaries and yet allot, as we have done, forty million pounds for productive projects? What would have happened if we had opened the coffers of the Treasury of the State, as they had done, and distributed their contents among officials and let come what may thereafter? The year that ensued would have found the Government unable to pay the salaries of officials.

"How easy it would have been to satisfy all those malcontents! but what is the price that our country would pay out of its hopes and its future for that satisfaction?

"Such is the role that history has fixed for us. We cannot escape from it however high is the price we pay. We never misunderstood this role, or the nature of the duties it imposed upon us. These are steps to redress the wrongs of the past and clear away the deposits. We have gone ahead with them and have suffered hardships for their sake.

"As for the future, it is not for us only to speak. In order to safeguard political life we have resorted to several leaders of public opinion of various classes and creeds. We said to them, 'Draw up a constitution which will safeguard the country's sacred heritage'; and hence the Commission of the Constitution.

" In order to guarantee economic life in future we sought the most eminent professors in the country and said to them, ' Plan prosperity for the country and ensure for every citizen his daily crust of bread '; and hence the Council of National Production.

" These are our limits which we have not transgressed. To remove the rocks and the obstacles that block the way at whatever price is our duty. The way is open to whoever has ideas and experience to contribute to the future in all its aspects. It is a duty imperative upon us all. We must not be selfish and monopolize it. Our mission necessitates that we should unite them all for the sake of Egypt, Egypt the strong, Egypt the free.

" We should first of all agree upon one thing before we proceed further with this discourse and that is to define the boundaries of place as far as we are concerned. If I were told that our place is the capital we live in I beg to differ. If I were told that our place is limited by the political boundaries of our country I also do not agree. If our problem, as a whole, is confined within our capital or inside our political boundaries, it will be easy. We would lock ourselves, close all the doors and live in an ivory tower away as much as possible from the world, its complications, its wars and crises. All these crash through the gates of our country and leave their effects upon us though we have nothing to do with them.

" The era of isolation is now gone. Gone are also the days when barbed wires marked the frontiers separating and isolating countries, and every country must look beyond its frontiers to find out where the currents that affected it spring, how it should live with others. . . etc. It has become imperative that every country should look around itself to find out its position and its environment and decide what it can do, what its vital sphere is and where the scene of its activity and what its positive role could be in this troubled world.

" As I often sit in my study and think quickly of this subject I ask myself, ' What is our positive role in this troubled world and where is the scene, in which we can play that role? '

" I survey our conditions and find out we are in a group of circles which should be the theatre of our activity and in which we try to move as much as we can.

" Fate does not play jokes. Events are not produced haphazardly. Existence cannot come out of nothing.

" We cannot look stupidly at a map of the world not realizing our place therein and the role determined to us by that place. Neither can we ignore that there is an Arab circle surrounding us and that this circle is as much a part of us as we are a part of it, that our history has been mixed with it and that its interests are linked with ours. These are actual facts and not mere words.

"Can we ignore that there is a continent of Africa in which fate has placed us and which is destined to-day to witness a terrible struggle on its future? This struggle will affect us whether we want or not.

Can we ignore that there is a Moslem world with which we are tied by bonds which are not only forged by religious faith but also tightened by the facts of history. I said once that fate plays no jokes. It is not in vain that our country lies to the South-west of Asia close to the Arab world, whose life is intermingled with ours. It is not in vain that our country lies in the North-east of Africa, a position from which it gives upon the dark continent wherein rages to-day the most violent struggle between white colonizers and black natives for the possession of its inexhaustible resources. It is not in vain that Islamic civilization and Islamic heritage, which the Mongols ravaged in their conquest of the old Islamic capitals, retreated and sought refuge in Egypt where they found shelter and safety as a result of the counter-attack with which Egypt repelled the invasion of these Tartars at Ein Galout.

"All these are fundamental facts, whose roots lie deeply in our life; whatever we do, we cannot forget them or run away from them.

"I see no reason why, as I sit alone in my study with my thoughts wandering away, I should recall, at this stage of my thinking, a well-known story by the Italian poet Luigi Pirandello which he called, "Six Characters in Search of an Author".

"The annals of history are full of heroes who carved for themselves great and heroic roles and played them on momentous occasions on the stage. History is also charged with great heroic roles which do not find actors to play them on the stage. I do not know why I always imagine that in this region in which we live there is a role wandering aimlessly about seeking an actor to play it. I do not know why this role, tired of roaming about in this vast region which extends to every place around us, should at last settle down, weary and worn out, on our frontiers beckoning us to move, to dress up for it and to perform it since there is nobody else who can do so.

"Here I hasten to point out that this role is not a leading role. It is one of interplay of reactions and experiments with all these factors aiming at exploding this terrific energy latent in every sphere around us and at the creation, in this region, of a tremendous power capable of lifting this region up and making it play its positive role in the construction of the future of humanity.

"There is no doubt that the Arab circle is the most important and the most closely connected with us. Its history merges with ours. We have suffered the same hardships, lived the same crises and when we fell prostrate under the spikes of the horses of conquerors they lay with us.

"Religion also fused this circle with us. The centres of religious enlightenment radiated from Mecca, from Koufa and later from Cairo.

"These were also collected in an environment in which all these historic, spiritual and material factors are closely knitted. As far as I am concerned I remember that the first elements of Arab consciousness began to filter into my mind as a student in secondary schools, wherefrom I went out with my fellow schoolboys on strike on December 2nd of every year as a protest against the Balfour Declaration whereby England gave the Jews a national home usurped unjustly from its legal owners.

"When I asked myself at that time why I left my school enthusiastically and why I was angry for this land which I never saw, I could not find an answer except the echoes of sentiment. Later a form of comprehension of this subject began when I was a cadet in the Military College studying the Palestine campaigns in particular and the history and conditions of this region in general which rendered it, throughout the last century, an easy prey ravaged by the claws of a pack of hungry beasts.

"My comprehension began to be clearer as the foundation of its facts stood out when I began to study, as a student in the Staff College, the Palestine campaign and the problems of the Mediterranean in great detail.

"And when the Palestine crisis loomed on the horizon I was firmly convinced that the fighting in Palestine was not fighting on a foreign territory. Nor was it inspired by sentiment. It was a duty imposed by self-defence.

"I remember one day, after the partition of Palestine was declared in September 1947, the Liberal Officers held a meeting, during which they decided to assist the resistance movement in Palestine. The next day I went to the house of Hadj Amin El Husseini, the Mufti of Palestine who lived in Zeitoun then. I said to him ,'You need officers to direct battles, and to train volunteers. These are a great number of officers some in the Egyptian Army who would like to volunteer. They are at your disposal any time you require.' Hadji Amin expressed admiration of the spirit but he thought he would ask permission of the Egyptian Government before he said anything. He said to me, 'I shall give you my reply after I have received the permission of the Egyptian Government.' I went back to him after a few days. The answer he recieved from the Egyptian Government was refusal.

"But we did not remain silent. Later the artillery of Ahmed Abdel Aziz began to hammer the Jewish colonies south of Jerusalem. The artillery officer in charge was Kamal El Dine Hussein, a member of the constituent committee of the Liberal Officers, which has now become the Council of the Revolution.

"I also recall another secret which was the most valued by the Liberal Officers. Hassan Ibrahim had left for Damascus, where he contacted some officers of Fawzy El Kawookgy. El Kawookgy was then the commander of the forces of Arab Liberation, and was preparing a decisive battle in the northern zone of Palestine. Hassan Ibrahim and Abdel Latif El Baghdadi planned an audacious plan for a decisive action in the battle, for which the Liberation forces were then preparing. The main lines of this plan were: That the Arab Liberation Forces had no planes to support them in the battle and tilt the balance of victory in their favour. Had they had a supporting force from the air, which would bombard the focus of the operation from above, it would have been a deciding factor. But where could the Liberation Forces get the planes to fulfil this dream?

"Hassan Ibrahim and Abdul Latif El Baghdadi did not hesitate to mention that the Egyptian Air Force should perform this assignment. But how? Egypt was not yet in the Palestine War. Supervision over the armed forces, including the Air Force, was close and alert. Yet despair could not penetrate into the details of this plan. A wonderful movement began in the aerodrome of the Air Force. Tremendous energy for the repair and the preparation of planes was noticeable. Remarkable efforts for training and exercise spread like wildfire among the pilots; and very few knew the secret. Those who did, understood that the planes and the pilots were getting ready for the day when a secret signal would come from Syria. They would then fly full out to take part in the decisive battle for the Holy Land. They would then proceed to an aerodrome near Damascus where they would land and wait the repercussion in Egypt and hear the echoes of this movement they embarked upon; after that they would decide which course to take. The most favourable possibility was that every pilot who took part in the operation, would be court-martialled. Many had already planned their lives if circumstances stood between them and the return to the Mother Country for a number of years.

"The feeling of the Executive Committee of the Liberal Officers, which was emphatically the feeling which every pilot who took part in this daring plan entertained, was neither love of adventure nor a reaction of the sentiment. It was a remarkable consciousness of our fate that Rafah was not the last boundary of our country, and that our sphere of security compels us to defend the frontiers of our brethren, with whom we were destined to live together in one region.

"The plan did not materialize then because we did not get the secret signal from Syria. Later, circumstances necessitated that all Arab Armies should enter the Palestine War.

"I do not want now to discuss the details of the Palestine War. This is a subject that needs several many-sided discussions. But one strange lesson of the Palestine War I care to mention: The Arab nations entered the Palestine War with the same degree of enthusiasm. They all shared the same feelings and had known quite well the limits of their security. They came out of the war with the same bitterness and frustration. Everyone of them was thus exposed, in its own country, to the same factors and was governed by the same forces, that caused their defeat; and made them bow their heads low with shame and humiliation.

"I sat by myself several times in the trenches and dug-outs of Iraq-el-Manshia. I was then the staff-officer of the sixth company, which held this sector, defended it sometimes and used it for attack often.

"I used to walk amidst the ruins all around me, which were left after the bombardments of the enemy. There I travelled far in my imagination. My voyage took me to the sphere of the stars where I would regard the whole area from my great height above. The picture lay before me at that time quite clear. Here was the place, wherein we lay beseiged. There were the posts of our company and those of other companies, that shared the same lines with us. Beyond were the enemy forces surrounding us. In other places there were other forces of ours besieged also and unable to move, and had space only to manœuvre on a small scale.

"The political circumstances prevailing in the capital from whence we received our orders threw round them all a siege more effective and paralysed us more than anything the enemy could do to us, who lay at Falouga.

"There were also the forces of our brothers-in-arms in the big Homeland, in the common interest and the motive that sent us rushing to the land of Palestine. There were the armies of our brethren, which were also our armies: all were besieged by the circumstances that surrounded them and their Governments. They all seemed like pawns in a game of chess, powerless and without will, except in so far as the hands of players move them.

"All our nations seemed, beyond our rear-lines, the victims of a tightly-woven conspiracy which deliberately concealed from their eyes the facts of events and misguided them beyond self-recognition.

"From the height of the stars above I used to come down to earth often and feel that I really defended my home and my children. Neither my dreams, the capitals, the States, the peoples, nor history meant anything to me then. This was how I felt when, in my wanderings, I came upon the children of refugees who were caught in the tentacles of the siege after their homes had been demolished and their property lost. I particularly remember a young girl of the same age as my daughter. I saw her rushing out, amidst danger and stray bullets and, bitten by the pangs of hunger and cold, looking for a crust of bread or a rag of cloth. I always said to myself, 'This may happen to my daughter.' I believe that what was happening in Palestine could happen, and may still happen to-day, in any part of this region. As long as it resigns itself to the factors and the forces which dominate now.

"After the siege and the battles in Palestine I came home with the whole region in my mind one complete whole. The events that followed confirmed this belief in me. As I pursued the developments of the situation I found nothing but echoes responding one to the other. An event may happen in Cairo to-day; it is repeated in Damascus, Beirut, Amman or any other place to-morrow. This was naturally in conformity with the picture that experience has left within me: One region, the same factors and circumstances, even the same forces opposing them all. It was clear that Imperialism was the most prominent of these forces; even Israel itself was but one of the outcomes of Imperialism. If it had not fallen under British mandate Zionism could not have found the necessary support to realize the idea of a national home in Palestine. That idea would have remained a foolish vision, practically hopeless.

"As I put down these impressions, I have before me the memoirs of Hayem Weizemann, the President of the Republic of Israel and its real founder. These memoirs were published in his famous book called *Trial and Error*. They contain certain passages worthy of consideration on account of the particular stamp they bear. I pause at the following: 'It was essential,' Weizemann wrote, 'that a Big Power should assist us. There were two great Powers in the world who could give us this assistance; Germany and Britain.

"'As for Germany it preferred to keep away and avoid any intervention. Britain was sympathetic and patronizing.' Again I pause as I behold Weizemann saying, 'It happened during the Sixth Zionist Conference which we held in Switzerland that Hertzel stood declaring that Great Britain only, of all the States of the world, has recognized the Jews as a nation in an independent form and apart from others. "We, the Jews," he continued, "are worthy of having a home and being a State." Hertzel then read a letter to that effect from Lord Latterson on behalf of the British Government. In this letter Lord Latterson offered us the territory of Uganda to be a National Home.[1] The members of the Conference accepted the offer. After that we suppressed and checkmated this proposal at its early stage and buried it without clamour. Britain again sought to satisfy us. After this proposal we formed a commission of a considerable number of Jewish savants, who proceeded to Cairo to study the territory of Sinai. There they met Lord Cromer, who sympathized with our aspiration to achieve a National Home. Later, I met Lord Balfour, the British Foreign Secretary, who hastened to ask me, "Why didn't you accept Uganda as a National Home?" I replied, that Zionism is a national and political movement is true, but there is also the spiritual side which we cannot overlook. I am certain that if we ignore this spiritual aspect

[1] Uganda is the great British protectorate (98,000 square miles) adjoining the Sudan. It is prosperous on account of its coffee and cotton crops.

we shall not be able to realize our political and national vision. I also asked Balfour, "What would you do if somebody would suggest you take Paris instead of London? Would you accept?"'

"I also ponder over another passage in Weizemann: 'In the autumn of 1921 I returned to London where I was called to supervise the drafting of the covenant of the British Mandate in Palestine. The rough draft should have been submitted to the League of Nations in order that it might adopt a resolution upon it. Afterwards the Conference of St. Remo approved the very idea of the Mandate.

"'Lord Curzon had then replaced Lord Balfour as Foreign Secretary and he was responsible for the drafting of the covenant. With us in London then was the great jurist Ibn Cohen, one of the ablest authors of legal formulae in the world. Eric Adam, Curson's secretary, also co-operated with us. We had a difference with Curzon, a difference which was the first and last.

"'We had recorded in the draft of the covenant a clause pledging Britain to the Balfour Declaration. And demanding that its policy in Palestine should be on the basis of a National Home for the Jews. The text of the clause we wrote was as follows: "And the recognition of the historic rights of the Jews in Palestine." Curzon proposed that this clause should be toned down so as not to arouse the Arabs when they read it. He proposed it should read: "And the recognition of the connections of the Jews and their historic relations with Palestine."'

"I wish to continue quoting from Weizemann's *Trial and Error*, but we know that these old incidents were the first germs of the dreadful repercussions that tore Palestine into shreds and destroyed its very existence.

"I now revert to what I was discussing, namely, that Imperialism is the great force that throws around the whole region a fatal siege a hundred times stricter and more cruel than the siege around us in Falouga or around our armies and our governments in their capitals, from whence we received our orders.

"I thus began to believe after these facts became established within me, in one common struggle and repeat to myself, 'As long as the region is one, and its conditions, its problems and its future, and even the enemy are the same, however different are the masks that the enemy covers its face with, why should we dissipate our efforts? The experience of what followed July 23rd increased my faith in a united struggle and its necessity. The secret of the picture began to reveal itself and the darkness which shrouded its details began to disappear.

"I confess I also begin to visualize the great obstacles that blocked the way of a united struggle. But I also believe that these stumbling blocks should be removed because they are the work of the one and the same enemy. I commenced lately a series of political contacts with the object of unifying the struggle whatever is the means. I came out of these contacts with an important result, namely, that the primary obstacle in our path is 'suspicion'. The seeds of that suspicion were sown in us by the common enemy in order to stand between us and the united struggle.

"I recollect that one day I sat talking with an Arab politician and a colleague of his. As he replied to me he turned to his colleague to find out the effects of his answer before he tried to discover its result on me. I said to him, 'Overcome all suspicion you have and pour out to me all the contents of your heart; look me in the face and regard me in the eye.' I do not mean to lighten the obstacles that lie between us and the unification of the struggle. Some of them are intricate and have roots deep in the environment and the historical and geographical circumstances which involve them. But is it certain that with a certain amount of elasticity, derived from far-sightedness and not from negligence, we may find the position we should all take without embarrassment or pertinacity in order to face the united struggle?

"I do not hesitate for one moment to mention that our united struggle would achieve for us and our peoples everything we wish and aspire to; I shall always go on saying that we are strong, but the great catastrophe is that we do not know the extent of our strength.

"We make a mistake in our definition of power. Power is not merely shouting aloud. Power is to act positively with all the components of power.

"When I attempt to analyse the components of our power I cannot help but point out three principal forces of power which should be the first to be taken into account.

"The first source is that we are a group of neighbouring peoples joined together with such spiritual and material bonds as can ever join any group of peoples. Our peoples have traits, components and civilization, in whose atmosphere the three sacred and heavenly creeds have originated. This cannot be altogether ignored in any effort at reconstructing a stable world in which peace prevails.

"As for the second source it is our territory itself and the position it has on the map of the world, that important strategic situation which can be rightly considered the meeting-place, the crossroad and the military corridor of the world.

"The third source is petroleum, which is the vital nerve of civilization, without which all its means cannot possibly exist, whether huge works for production, modes of communication by land, sea and air, weapons of war whether they are planes flying above the clouds or submarines submerged under layers of water. All these, without petroleum, would become mere pieces of iron, rusty, motionless and lifeless.

"I wish I could linger a while and discuss petroleum. Its existence, as a material fact established by statistics and figures, is worth making it a model for a discussion of the importance of the sources of power in our countries.

"I have read lately a treatise published by Chicago University on the state of petroleum. I wish every individual of our people could read it, ponder upon its meanings and give free play to his mind to realize the great significance which lies behind figures and statistics. This treatise shows, for example, that to extract the petrol of Arab countries would not cost a great deal of money.

"Petrol companies have spent sixty million dollars in Colombia since 1916 and have not found a drop of oil until 1936. These companies also spent forty-four million dollars in Venezuela and did not find a drop of oil until after fifteen years.

"These companies again spent thirty million dollars in the Dutch East Indies and have not struck oil until very recently.

"The final result which this treatise proved in this subject is as follows:

"The capital necessary for extracting one barrel of petrol in the Arab countries is ten cents; the centre of oil production has shifted from the U.S.A., where oil wells have been exhausted, where the price of land is exorbitant, and where wages of workers are high, to the Arab territory, where the wells are untouched and in a virgin state, where expensive land can be had for nothing and where labour accepts subsistent wages.

"It is a fact that half the world's reserve of petroleum is still underground in the Arab regions and the second half is distributed

dreaming of a new life, firm believers that they have a place under the sun which they should occupy for life.'

"I recall I expressed some of these sentiments to His Majesty King Saud. He said to me, 'This is the real wisdom of the pilgrimage.' Verily I cannot visualize a higher wisdom.

"When my mind travelled to the eighty million Moslems in Indonesia, the fifty in China and the several other million in Malaya, Siam and Burma and the hundred million in Pakistan, the hundred million or more in the Middle East and the forty in Russia, as well as the other millions in the distant parts of the world, when I visualize these millions united in one faith I have a great consciousness of the tremendous potentialities that co-operation amongst them all can achieve: a co-operation that does not deprive them of their loyalty to their countries, but which guarantees for them and their brethren a limitless power.

"I now revert to the wandering role that seeks an actor to perform it. Such is the role, such are its features and such is its stage.

"We, and only we, are impelled by our environment and are capable of performing this role."

NOTE. On this note Nasser ends his extraordinary testament. Colonel Nasser has denied that he has any plans to link Egypt with Arab oil wealth, but his remarks on Arab oil I find illuminating.

There is no doubting the immensity of the vision that rides from one Moslem frontier to another. Africa, China, Siam, Burma, Malaya, Pakistan, even the Soviet Union, all have great Moslem populations.

The idea has been conceived. It is for us to watch its unfolding in political events.

INDEX

INDEX

To the Reader